Rural tensions in nineteenth-century Knock, County Mayo

Maynooth Studies in Local History

SERIES EDITOR Raymond Gillespie

This volume is one of five short books published in the Maynooth Studies in Local History series in 2021. Like their predecessors they range widely over the local experience in the Irish past. Chronologically they range across the 19th century and into the 20th century but they focus on problems that reappeared in almost every period of Irish history. They chronicle the experiences of individuals grappling with their world from the Cork surgeon, Denis Brenan Bullen, in the early 19th century to the politician and GAA administrator Peadar Cowan in the 20th century. From a different perspective they resurrect whole societies under stress from the rural tensions in Knock, Co. Mayo, to the impact of the Famine on Sir William Palmer's estates in Mayo. A rather different sort of institution under stress, Dublin's cattle market, provides the framework for charting the final years of the world that depended on that institution. Geographically they range across the length of the country from Dublin to Cork and westwards into Mayo. Socially they move from those living on the margins of society in Knock through to the prosperous world of the social elite in Cork. In doing so they reveal diverse and complicated societies that created the local past and present the range of possibilities open to anyone interested in studying that past. Those possibilities involve the dissection of the local experience in the complex and contested social worlds of which it is part as people strove to preserve and enhance their positions within their local societies. It also reveals the forces that made for cohesion in local communities and those that drove people apart, whether through large scale rebellion or through acts of inter-personal violence. Such studies of local worlds over such long periods are vital for the future since they not only stretch the historical imagination but provide a longer perspective on the evolution of society in Ireland and help us to understand more fully the complex evolution of the Irish experience. These works do not simply chronicle events relating to an area within administrative or geographically determined boundaries, but open the possibility of understanding how and why particular regions had their own personality in the past. Such an exercise is clearly one of the most exciting challenges for the future and demonstrates the vitality of the study of local history in Ireland.

Like their predecessors, these five short books are reconstructions of the socially diverse worlds of the poor as well as the rich, women as well as men, the geographical marginal of Mayo as well as those located near the centre of power. They reconstruct the way in which those who inhabited those worlds lived their daily lives, often little affected by the large themes that dominate the writing of national history. In addressing these issues, studies such as those presented in these short books, together with their predecessors, are at the forefront of Irish historical research and represent some of the most innovative and exciting work being undertaken in Irish history today. They also provide models that others can follow up and adapt in their own studies of the Irish past. In such ways will we understand better the regional diversity of Ireland and the social and cultural basis for that diversity. They, with their predecessors, convey the vibrancy and excitement of the world of Irish local history today.

Maynooth Studies in Local History: Number 152

Rural tensions in nineteenth-century Knock, County Mayo

Land, landlords and the archdeacon

Frank Mayes

FOUR COURTS PRESS

Set in 10pt on 12pt Bembo by
Carrigboy Typesetting Services for
FOUR COURTS PRESS LTD
7 Malpas Street, Dublin 8, Ireland
www.fourcourtspress.ie
and in North America for
FOUR COURTS PRESS
c/o IPG, 814 N Franklin St, Chicago, IL 60610

ISBN 978–1–84682–971–0

Printed in Ireland
by SprintPrint, Dublin.

Contents

Acknowledgments

This study is based on a thesis submitted in partial fulfilment for a MA degree in Irish History from the National University of Ireland, Maynooth, 2020.[1] My thanks are due to the staff and students of Maynooth University who encouraged me in my research. In particular, I am especially grateful for the help given by my supervisor, Dr Jacinta Prunty, and by Professor Raymond Gillespie.

My appreciation goes also to the staff of the institutions visited during the course of this study, namely Maynooth University Library, the McClay Library QUB, the National Archives of Ireland, the National Library of Ireland, and the Valuation Office.

I am also thankful for the ability, as a senior citizen, to travel on Irish Rail and Northern Ireland Railways without charge, which enabled me to travel from my home in Tyrone to Maynooth and arrive in plenty of time for eleven o'clock lectures! My thanks to the legislators, in both jurisdictions, who facilitated this progressive scheme.

Finally, my love and thanks to my wife, Bríd, for her unselfish support, patience and encouragement.

Introduction

Most studies of the relationship between landlords and their tenants, and in particular of the 'land war' that broke out after the formation of the National Land League in October 1879, have concentrated on the national picture.[1] More local studies, such as those of Donnelly or Jordan, have studied the situation at a county level.[2] The aim of my study is to investigate the tensions within a rural community at this time, at the parish, or even townland level. Where better to do this than in the parish of Knock, Co. Mayo? The apparition that some parishioners reportedly saw on 21 August 1879 brought both national and international attention to the village. Yet on the night in question only some of the inhabitants chose to view the spectacle. Not even Archdeacon Bartholomew Cavanagh, Knock's parish priest, when he was told by his housekeeper, chose to go and see what was happening.

On 25 May 1879, Father Cavanagh had preached a sermon in which he condemned aspects of the Mayo land movement that was to become the Irish Land League later that year. The movement had held its first meeting in Irishtown, just a few miles from Knock, only a month previously. The movement's response was to call a meeting in Knock the following Sunday (1 June) to protest against the cleric and his views. The *Connaught Telegraph* newspaper estimated that 20,000–30,000 people converged on the village.[3] The police were also present, and a confidential report was compiled for the chief secretary in Dublin Castle.[4] This report estimated the crowd as 1,500, just a fraction of the figure given by the *Connaught Telegraph*, but still enormous for a village of about 30 houses and less than 200 people. The meeting accused the priest of shielding some landlords who were not amenable to the demands of the tenant farmers. This surely points to some kind of tension within the community.

The thesis on which this study is based also investigated whether the technique known as 'family reconstitution', which has been used by some English local historians, could be adapted for use in the Irish context.[5] Family reconstitution was originally developed, in the English context, by the Cambridge Group for the History of Population and Social Structure led by E.A. Wrigley and R. Schofield. They used parish registers to obtain demographic data, such as marriage age or life expectancy. Similar methods have also been used by social historians such as Wrightson and Levine or Reay to produce histories of individual communities at the hamlet, town or parish level.[6] Such 'total reconstitution methods' used other primary sources such as censuses, poll books, newspapers and, indeed, any other source that might shed more light on family or kinship relationships within a community.

The first chapter of this study will examine the social history of the parish of Knock. Daniel Campbell, who was born in Knock in 1825, and who left the parish for England in 1849, has left a recollection of his time in the parish, which confirms that tensions did indeed exist within it while he was living there.[7] He specifically mentions 'factions' within the community, without actually stating what or who were involved.[8]

The following chapter will examine the tensions that may have existed within the community of Knock between the end of the Famine, when Campbell left, and 1879 when Knock witnessed not only an apparition, but also the start of the 'land war'. It discusses the relationship between landlords and tenants as well as the tensions among the tenant-farmers themselves; between large cattle farmers (the ranchers), and the small subsistent and tillage farmers. Until the 1970s the historiography of the land question in Ireland was probably best exemplified by Pomfret who portrayed the 'struggle' of an oppressed Catholic tenantry to overthrow the ruthless, aristocratic (and often absent) landlord class.[9] This orthodoxy was challenged by Barbara Solow and James Donnelly whose more nuanced approaches suggested that, between the Famine and the land war, rents were generally low and evictions relatively rare (especially after the mid-1850s) and that ruthless and uncaring landlords were the exception rather than the rule.[10] Agricultural prices, especially of cattle as opposed to tillage crops, rose during this period. This was despite an agricultural depression in the early 1860s. While rents also rose, they did so at a rate that was seemingly less, in most cases, than the tenants' income, especially for those tenants with larger holdings. This led Donnelly to conclude that the land war was a 'revolution of rising expectations'.[11] The works of Bew and Clark have demolished the myth of a homogeneous and united tenantry.[12] The outlook and interests of large cattle farmers, small-holders and landless labourers were different and, not infrequently, in conflict. For an examination of the tension at a local level one can turn to Donald E. Jordan who used Co. Mayo, the cradle of the Land League, as his study area.[13] He argues that studies

> based upon analyses of social and economic change on the provincial or national level ... can illuminate major economic trends, but necessarily distorts economic and social organization at the local level, where the battle between landlords and their tenants was actually waged. Consequently, the questions ... raised by Bew's and Clark's studies can best be answered through an exposition of the complexities of local Irish society.[14]

One of the aims of the present study is to attempt to bring the local 'level' down one step further to examine such events within a parish or even a townland.

A 'devotional revolution' was experienced by the Catholic Church in the 1850s which subsequently saw an increase in mass attendance and a large increase in the number of clergy and nuns ministering to the population.[15] This did not eliminate tensions within the community however. At the national level Archbishop (later Cardinal) Cullen, archbishop of Dublin, 'who until his death in 1878 dominated Irish Catholicism, had to exercise his authority over the priesthood with great care.'[16] He did, however, manage to stamp his (and Rome's) authority on the church. According to Barr: 'In re-engergizing his church, Cullen created modern Irish Catholicism out of the wreckage of famine and internal division. Paul Cullen did not make the great mass of the Irish people into practising Catholics, but he went a long way towards making them Roman Catholics'.[17] Knock parish is in the diocese of Tuam and Archbishop MacHale, its archbishop from 1834 until his death in 1881, was a much more strident 'nationalist' than Cullen. The two men clashed over many issues, but within his own diocese MacHale had an almost saint-like reputation.[18] Parish priests and their curates were also involved in many aspects of the political, social and economic life of their community, so that, according to Foster, Cardinal Cullen

> presided over a Church that was violently engagé in local politics, controlling, for instance, a quarter of the votes in Kinsale, working with the drink interest at Waterford, defying the hierarchy by celebrating mass for a dead Fenian in one place, or by backing a Tory candidate in another … Priests and people were often locked in conflict, but the priest's political role was generally accepted: a sign of the confessional nature of Irish life.[19]

Archdeacon Cavanagh, Knock's parish priest, clashed with the land movement. What were relationships like between the clergy and parishioners at Knock? What effect did the changes that occurred during the period under study have on Cavanagh's flock at Knock? What were the relationships between clergy and the landlords? Was proselytism a problem?

1. The 1901 census as a source of 19th-century social history

The Irish census of 1901 is an underutilized resource for the study of the country during the 19th century. In the thesis on which this study is based, the census together with other primary sources such as will calendars, newspapers, school registers and valuation records, were used to attempt a total family reconstitution of the families living in the townlands of Drum and Carrowmore, the townlands comprising the small village of Knock in the second half of the 19th century.

The exercise was not successful since a complete reconstitution was not possible in any of the 60 families examined from Knock, but that does not exclude analysis of the census data to illuminate various aspects of Knock society at the end of the 19th century including:

1 age structures of the population
2 literacy: the proportion and ages of those who could read and/or write
3 language: the proportion and ages of Irish and English speakers
4 kinship and household structures. Were families nuclear or complex?

For the purpose of this analysis, the 1901 census data was expanded from just two townlands to the entire civil parish of Knock. The records themselves, including the householder returns, are in the National Archives and are available online.[1] Knock civil parish consists of 45 townlands distributed between three District Electoral Divisions (DEDs): Knock North, Knock South and Ballyhowly, all within the Claremorris Poor Law Union. As with any historical document the 1901 census should be evaluated to assess its accuracy and completeness. Questions that must be addressed include: how accurately were the ages recorded? How consistent were the enumerators? Is the relationship to the head of the family ambiguous? For example, a lodger who was also a relative may be recorded as either. It seems likely that, in this case, any such inaccuracies or omissions will have been random and there was no systematic misrepresentation of the reality.

The data, as recorded in the household returns (Form A), were extracted for the Knock townlands and transferred to an Excel spreadsheet. The dataset was then interrogated to help illuminate some of the possible social tensions that may have been operating in the village of Knock in the latter half of the nineteenth century, and which will be discussed fully in subsequent chapters.

THE AGE STRUCTURE OF THE POPULATION

The total population of Knock parish, as enumerated by the household return forms in 1901, was 2,824 people, 1,458 females and 1,366 males. All inhabitants were described as 'Catholic' or 'Roman Catholic' (in a variety of spellings) with no other religions represented. The summary data for this census, published in 1902, gives the population of the parish as 2,806, 1,357 males and 1,449 females, with two people, one male and one female recorded as Protestant and Episcopalian, with the remainder recorded as Catholic.[2] The reason for these discrepancies is unclear.

A population pyramid was constructed from the age structures of the population (Figure 1). A spike in numbers for those age intervals which contain a zero (especially 40 and 60) suggests that some inhabitants were approximating their ages to the nearest ten-year age. Such a hypothesis is supported by Figure 2. For those inhabitants with stated ages between 21 and 80, the average percentage change in the number of inhabitants with the same final digit in their age, compared to those one-year younger (e.g. numbers aged 54, 64, 74 etc., as a percentage of those aged 53, 63, 73 etc.) was calculated. Those who

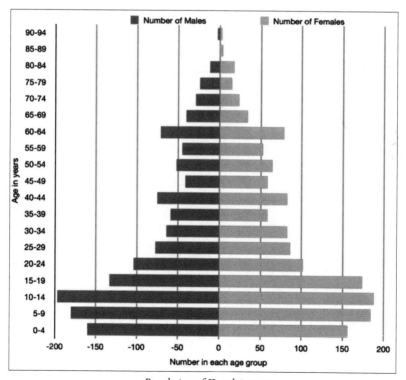

1. Population of Knock in 1901.
Source: Census of Ireland, 1901 (NAI, online at: https://genealogy.nationalarchives.ie)

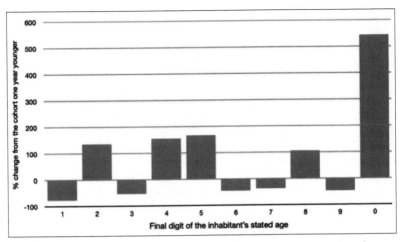

2. Population of Knock, 1901, arranged by the last digit of their stated age for
inhabitants aged between 21 and 80.
Source: Calculated from data in the Census of Ireland, 1901
(NAI, online at: https://genealogy.nationalarchives.ie)

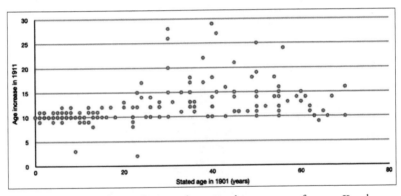

3. Stated age differences between the 1901 and 1911 censuses for some Knock
inhabitants living in the townlands of Drum and Carrowmore.
Source: Census of Ireland, 1901 and 1911 (NAI, online at: https://genealogy.nationalarchives.ie)

gave their age with a number ending in zero (i.e. 30, 40, 50, 60, 70, 80) were, on
average, 542.9 per cent more numerous than those whose stated age was one-
year younger. This clearly indicates that some inhabitants were approximating
their ages. Were they rounding up, or down, or both? To answer this question
the families living in two Knock townlands, Drum and Carrowmore, in 1901,
were traced in the same townlands in the 1911 census. For those identified in
1911, their stated age was compared with that given in the previous census.

The 1911 census was conducted on Sunday 2 April, 10 years and two days
after the 1901 census, so that the vast majority of inhabitants were actually ten

years older in 1911 with a few (about 2/365 = 0.55 per cent) 11 years older. Figure 3 shows the stated age difference between the two censuses. It can be clearly seen that many adults were rounding their ages up rather than down (in 1911) and this presumably was also the case in 1901. It also shows that some young children had apparently aged only a few years between 1901 and 1911. The reason for these anomalies was probably that the children were misidentified. I had assumed that people with the same forename and surname, living within the same family, for both censuses were the same person. It seems likely that these children recorded in 1901 had died before 1911 and that a subsequent child born to that family had been given the same forename as the dead child.[3]

The profile of the population also produced another anomaly. Comparing the number of parishioners with stated ages between 51 and 55 (Figure 4) only two people gave their age as 53 years old on census day in 1901, far fewer than previous or subsequent years. These two people would have been born between 1 April 1848 and 31 March 1849. These dates occur at the height of the Irish Famine which may explain this anomaly, but the exact cause could be due to a number of reasons. Was there an epidemic, famine fever perhaps, among newborn infants that year, or perhaps there was mass migration out of the parish by families with very young children? Population changes during and after the Famine will be discussed more fully in the next chapter.

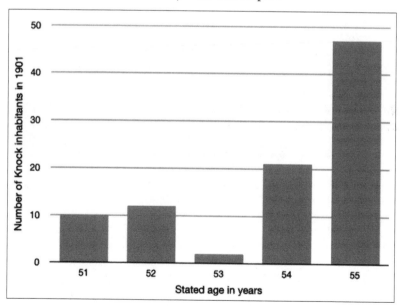

4. Numbers of inhabitants of Knock in 1901 with stated ages of between 51 and 55.
Source: Census of Ireland, 1901 (NAI, online at: https://genealogy.nationalarchives.ie)

LITERACY AMONG THE POPULATION

Under the column headed 'education' in the 1901 census, each inhabitant was required to 'state … whether he or she can "read and write", can "read only", or "cannot read"'.[4] For young children the enumerator often left this literacy column blank, presumably an indication that the child was not expected to be able to read or write. For those Knock inhabitants aged 11 or over only three had this column blank (or illegible). There were several variants to the answers given in the education column of the census. I have assumed that all answers, such as 'read only' or 'cannot write', that did not state 'can read and write' or just 'read and write', were not fully literate. For inhabitants aged between 11 and 20 (i.e., born between 1881 and 1890) the ability to read and write was almost 100 per cent, but for the older members of the population literacy declined with age before levelling off in those aged 56 and over (i.e., born before 1845 and starting school just after the Famine), when almost half of the population could read and write. This decline in literacy for inhabitants over the age of 11 is shown graphically in Figure 5.

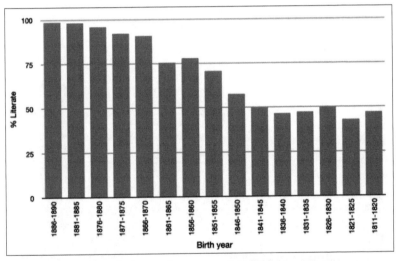

5. Decline in literacy with age among Knock inhabitants in 1901.
Source: Census of Ireland, 1901 (NAI, online at: https://genealogy.nationalarchives.ie)

It is known that there was at least one school in the parish since the 1830s and it is probable that most of the inhabitants, 98.8 per cent of whom gave their birthplace as 'Co. Mayo' went to these or neighbouring schools.[5]

LANGUAGES

The Irish-language column of Form A of the 1901 census states that the enumerator should: 'Write the word "IRISH" in this column opposite the name of each person who speaks IRISH *only,* and the words "IRISH & ENGLISH" opposite the names of those who can speak both languages. In other cases no entry should be made in this column.'[6]

In practice, however, the enumerators for Knock parish recorded the Irish language question in four categories: English, English and Irish, Irish and English, and Irish. One can assume 'English' means English only and that 'Irish' means Irish only and, indeed, some of these entries also contain the word 'only'. What about 'English and Irish' as opposed to 'Irish and English'? Does this indicate a person's first and second language? I believe that it does. John Blehein, a RIC constable, was the enumerator for some of Knock parish. He records many families as speaking 'English and Irish' and many others who speak 'Irish and English'. For example, in Drum townland, 60-year-old Dan Egan and his wife (and also some, but not all of their children) are listed as speaking 'English and Irish', whereas next door 63-year-old Michael McManus speaks 'Irish and English' as does Michael's other neighbour, 70-year-old Walter Kilduff and his wife Bridget.[7] It could be that Blehein and the other enumerators were listing the languages at random although they were always consistent in their ordering within families. It seems to me much more likely that they are recording the actual primary language rather than listing the order haphazardly.

Further investigation revealed that a total of six RIC men enumerated the parish. Blehein covered 14 townlands, sergeant F. Melamphy enumerated 16, whilst constables Micheal Fogerty, Charles Ward, James Dukelow and Phillip Egan were responsible for five, four, four, and one townland respectively.[8] Blehein, Melamphy, Fogerty and Ward all recorded both 'English and Irish' as well as 'Irish and English' bilingual speakers in Knock on census day but Dukelow and Egan, who were working on the southern tip of the parish, only recorded 'Irish and English' among the bilingual speakers. A check of neighbouring parishes revealed that both men enumerated outside of Knock parish. James Dukelow was responsible for several townlands in Kilcolman parish and, whilst the vast majority of his bilingual speakers were recorded as speaking 'Irish and English', he did record some as 'English and Irish' suggesting that he too was genuinely recording the primary and secondary languages of the population. Phillip Egan appears to be the exception. In addition to his one townland in Knock, he enumerated a further 20 townlands in Bekan and Annagh parishes for the 1901 census. He recorded every one of the hundreds of bilingual speakers as speaking 'Irish and English'. It is possible that the areas to which he was assigned had no bilingual speakers with English as their first language, but it is also possible that he was adhering strictly to the instruction on the census form to record bilingual speakers as 'Irish and English'.

Figure 6 was constructed on the assumption that, in Knock, bilingual speakers had their first language written first on the census form. It records how the proportion of the population of Knock with English as its first or only language varies with the reported age (and hence date of birth) of the population.

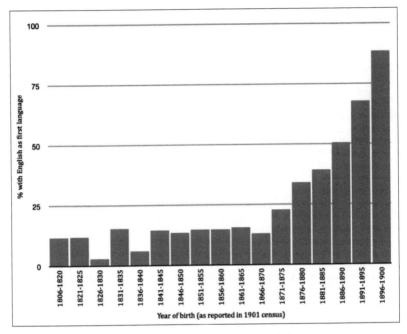

6. English as the first language amongst Knock inhabitants in 1901.
Source: Census of Ireland, 1901 (NAI, online at: https://genealogy.nationalarchives.ie)

For people living in Knock in 1901 who were born before 1870 about 20 per cent had English as a first language. For younger inhabitants the proportions rose steadily until, for those born in the 1880s almost all spoke predominantly English.

The reason for this sudden uptake of English is unclear. It was probably due to the uptake of national schooling, but the switch may have occurred at a later age or for other reasons.

KINSHIP AND HOUSEHOLD STRUCTURE

In what type of household did the people of Knock live? The 1901 census allows an examination of the types of households that existed there, and this gives us a snapshot of the family structures and kinship relationships that prevailed. Was the norm the two-generational nuclear family that we recognize today –

father, mother and children, or an extended multigenerational household that is believed to be the norm (sometimes incorrectly) in previous centuries?

The 61 families resident in the two townlands of Drum and Carrowmore in 1901 were classified into five categories:

1 nuclear families (a married couple with some or all of their children living with them).
2 couples (without children living with them).
3 complex families (a mixture of more complicated structures including extended families where a nuclear family is joined by another member(s) of their family or by employees such as servants or by lodgers or boarders. Other categories in this group are co-residing siblings and multiple families who are often a nuclear family where an adult offspring has married and started a family).
4 solitary individuals
5 others (often widows or widowers with some family members living with them).[9]

The percentages of families in each category is shown in Table 1.

Table 1. Family structure in Drum and Carrowmore townlands in 1901

Household Structure	Number of households	%
Nuclear	26	42.6
Couples	2	3.3
Complex	17	27.9
Solitary	2	3.3
Other	14	23.0
Total	61	100

Source: Census of Ireland, 1901 (NAI, online at: https://genealogy.nationalarchives.ie)

2. Knock, County Mayo, in the 19th century

Knock is a parish of 45 townlands comprising 11,704 acres in south-east Co. Mayo. In the 19th century, the parish was highly rural with no towns or villages until the latter part of the century. The townlands of Drum and Carrowmore, which are situated either side of the old Claremorris–Swinford road, coalesced into Knock village at about the time of the apparition. A newspaper report in 1884, describing the apparition, mentions that it occurred in 'the little village of Knock, near Claremorris'.[1] The 'village' at that time consisted of the Roman Catholic chapel, a boys' and a girls' primary school, together with a few roadside thatched cottages.

Only a few reports mentioned the parish in the first half of the century, indicating an out-of-the-way rural backwater in which not much of note happens. Lewis' (1837) *Topographical dictionary* entry is brief and to the point:

> Knock, or Knockdrumcalry, a parish, in the barony of COSTELLO, county of MAYO, and province of CONNAUGHT, five miles (E.) from Clare, on the road from Claremorrris to Swinford; containing 3036 inhabitants. It is chiefly under the improving system of tillage; there is a great quantity of bog.
>
> The principal seats are Ballyhoole, the residence of T. Rutledge, Esq.; and Aden, of A. O'Malley, Esq. It is a rectory and vicarage, in the diocese of Tuam, forming part of the union of Kiltullagh; the tithes amount to £37 13s. 10d.
>
> In the RC divisions it is the head of a union or district, comprising also the parish of Aughamore, in each of which is a chapel. There are six private schools, in which about 230 children are taught.[2]

Also dating from this pre-famine decade, Ordnance Survey officers sent letters back to Dublin describing the history, topography and antiquities of places surveyed. Knock is described in a letter sent by T. O'Conor, the distinguished antiquarian from a prominent Roscommon family. The letter was sent from Ballinrobe on 16 August 1838.

Knock Parish

The Irish name of this parish is Cnoc, a hill – <u>collis</u> – There is a church in ruins in it, on the South side wall of which near West gable is a doorway, constructed with cut stones, which is five ft. – 10 inches high, and three feet broad. In Caldragh townland, is <u>Tobar Keelain</u> holywell (Tobar Caolain) at which stations are performed on <u>Garland</u> Sunday. An old Castle stands in ruins in Ballyhowly townland (bealac cobla).[3]

As if to underline the paucity of history for the parish, O'Conor heads a page of his letter 'This page is left for any historical notices that may turn up, relating to Knock parish.'[4] Significantly, the rest of the page is blank.

THE POPULATION OF KNOCK PARISH, 1821–1901

The census of Ireland commenced in 1821. Summaries survive for the number of houses and people recorded at county, barony and parish levels for both 1821 and 1831. From 1841 onwards figures are also available for townlands. The 1821 and 1831 population totals have been severely criticized, but I have included them in Figures 7 and 8, which record the number of people and houses respectively in the parish between 1821 and 1901. The data before 1841 should therefore be treated with caution, but thereafter the figures are probably reliable.

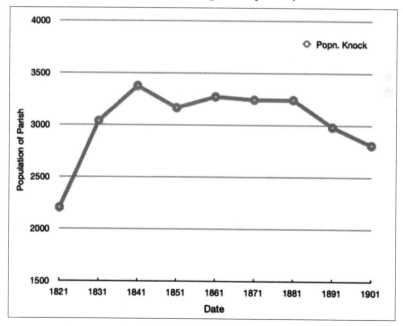

7. Population of Knock parish, 1821–1901.
Source: Censuses of population, 1821–1901 (see Appendix 1)

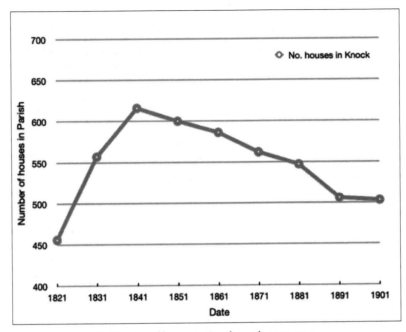

8. Number of houses in Knock parish, 1821–1901.
Source: Censuses of population, 1821–1901 (see Appendix 1)

The population of Knock parish increased during this period until 1851 when the catastrophic effects of the Famine, caused by the failure of the potato harvest in the years 1846 to 1850, resulted in a fall in the population. This fall was due to migration and deaths resulting from disease and malnutrition. The decline in the number of houses in Knock and its population compared with other places in Ireland between 1841 and 1901 is shown in Figures 9 and 10. It is clear that whilst the post-famine decline for Claremorris barony, Co. Mayo and Connacht was worse than the national average, Knock and Costello barony fared better than average.

This smaller decline in the population of Knock compared to other nearby parishes and the wider county of Mayo has been noted elsewhere. Hynes states 'there is no immediately obvious reasons why Knock had such a favourable outcome ... Indeed, there were good reasons to expect the opposite'.[5] He highlighted three possible explanations for this and paid particular attention to the fact that Knock parish falls within two baronies, Clanmorris and Costello. The Clanmorris part of the parish had a steeper decline than did that part in Costello barony but he makes no mention of the fact that Clanmorris barony, as a whole, had a steeper decline than did Costello (Fig. 10).

Explanations for this slower decline in the Knock population are 'exceptional landlord behaviour ... in-migration during the Famine ... and supernatural

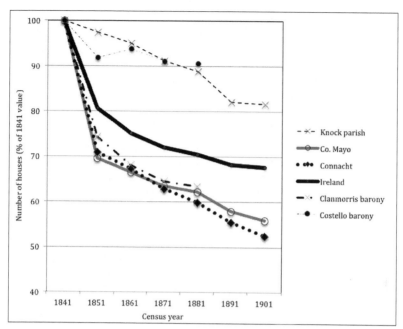

9. Number of houses recorded in the censuses, 1841–1901, for various Irish geographical land divisions.
Source: Censuses of population, 1841–1901 (see Appendix 1)

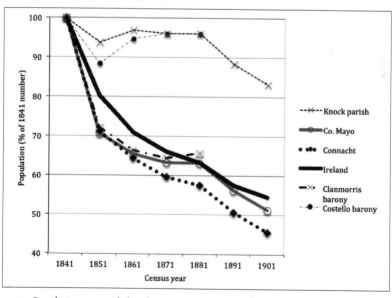

10. Population as recorded in the censuses, 1841–1901, for various Irish geographical and divisions.
Source: Censuses of population, 1841–1901 (see Appendix 1)

protection from famine fever.'[6] The exceptional landlord behaviour is based on the efforts of Charles Strickland, the agent on the Dillon estate throughout the Famine period. The Dillon estate was one of the largest in Ireland covering 83,749 acres of Mayo in 1876, as well as 5,435 acres in Roscommon and 136 acres in Westmeath.[7] Much of Knock but, importantly, not all of the parish was situated on the Dillon estate for the famine period and for the rest of the century. Charles Dillon, 14th Viscount Dillon, was described by his contempories as a 'most liberal and indulgent landlord.'[8] He inherited the Irish estates upon his father's death in 1832 and retained them, essentially intact, until his death in 1865. They then passed to his brother Theobald, the 15th Viscount. Both viscounts were absentee landlords, living on their principal estate in Oxfordshire, England. Dillon's 'big house' in Ireland was at Loughglynn in Tibohin townland in Frenchpark barony, Co. Roscommon. However it was the Strickland family, who were agents for the Dillons, who lived there for much of the 19th century. Charles Strickland, the agent during the famine period, was praised, both at the time and since, for his efforts in averting the effects of the Famine. He was chairman of the Ballaghaderreen town and Costello barony Relief Committee. He also served on the Gallen barony committee. He stated 'I have not thrown down a house or turned out a tenant from Lord Dillon's estate in all these distressed years. A few have given up their land but are left in their houses.'[9] In 1880, Finley Dun, *The Times* of London's correspondent, writing about the conditions in the west of Ireland, noted that during the famine on the Dillon estate, under Strickland's directions,

> thirteen stores were opened on various parts of the estate, and provisions sold at prime cost; the needy were freely helped. In favourable contrast to many other Irish estates there was consequently no serious destitution, no decimating famine fever, no great exodus of the survivors.[10]

The Relief Committee for Aughamore and Knock, meeting at Kilkelly on 26 June 1847, passed a resolution which they published in the press:

> Bearing testimony to Mr Strickland's very great and extraordinary exertions on behalf of the suffering poor, from the moment the awful visitation commenced to the present … We, in conclusion, beg to add, that were other large estates in this country managed with the same scrupulous regard to the several interests of both Landlord and Tenant, as those of Lord Dillon are, by Mr Strickland, the people of this country would not be in their present wretched state. By his strenuous efforts large quantities of provisions have been brought into the country – the markets have been kept down – meal sold indiscriminately to the tenants of all estates at cost price – hundreds relieved gratuitously; and, in fact, every exertion made to alleviate the suffering of the poor.[11]

The letter was signed by several Poor Law Guardians, including Knock landlord F.R. O'Grady as well as Patrick O'Grady, the parish priest of Knock and Aughamore, together with his curates Thomas Waters and Richard Prendergast. While these gentlemen may not have been representative of the entire population of Knock and Aughamore, it does, perhaps, indicate the affection that the Dillons, and especially Mr Strickland, were held in by the middle classes during the Famine.

In-migration from areas hardest hit by the Famine has been suggested by Jordan, based, in part, on the work of Cousens.[12] Jordan suggests that on the more fertile lands of central Mayo, many landless labourers and tenants on small, uneconomic holdings, who had become homeless, migrated to the poorer lands of eastern Mayo. Cousens argued that it was the availability of reclaimable wasteland in these eastern parts of the county that facilitated such relocations. Jordan concludes:

> in eastern Mayo land was reclaimed during the Famine and it seems reasonable to suggest that the people doing the reclamation had been evicted from land in the more fertile lowlands. In eastern Mayo they found land of marginal quality that held little incentive for landlord-initiated consolidation. The result was low Famine depopulation and rapid repopulation during the following decades.[13]

A full explanation of these complex issues of population changes during and following the Famine are still awaited. It is unresolved as to what factors were operating in the county which could explain the differences in population changes between 1841 and 1881. It is possible that landlord behaviour was one factor, but what about difference observed on a single estate (for example Dillon's)? Did the rundale system of land management play a part? Was the quality of land significant? What evidence is there of land reclamation or improvement during this period? Whatever factors were involved, Hynes is dismissive of the observations, research and analysis of commentators such as Coulter, Dun or Jordan, claiming that, for example, contemporary reporters' accounts of landlord benevolence were 'evidence of Dillon and Strickland's popular reputation more than of their behaviour during the Famine.'[14] His objections are more philosophical than practical, believing that 'outsiders' lack the 'insider's cultural framework' to ask the right questions when examining events such as these.[15]

One such insider was Daniel Campbell. According to Hynes, Campbell provides the third explanation for the slower rate of decline of the population of Knock parish after the Famine – supernatural protection from famine fever. Daniel Campbell, according to his own account, was born in the townland of Eden, Knock parish, in 1825. He left Ireland for England in 1849 and remained there for the rest of his life.[16] After the apparition at Knock in 1879 Campbell wrote a manuscript account of his recollections of the parish before the Famine.[17] The manuscript is now lost, but a typescript was made by Fr John Byrne, CP, from the original loaned to him by Campbell's grandson, Revd Phillip Brennan, CP.[18] The typescript is undated but the National Library of Ireland has catalogued it as 'Typescript copy of manuscript history of the parish of Knock, Co. Mayo, 1900?' The manuscript can be dated to between March 1880, when a list of cures, referred to by Campbell, was published in the press and 23 January 1885 when Campbell died.[19] If he was aware of the death in November 1881 of Archbishop McHale, who officiated at Campbell's first communion and who Campbell refers to as the present archbishop, then the time frame can be narrowed further. In either case Campbell's 'history' is clearly a recollection of his life in Knock in the light of the apparition in 1879. Indeed, Campbell entitles the document 'Apparition of the Blessed Virgin at the Chapel at Knock'.

Eugene Hynes, in his book *Knock; the Virgin's apparition*, devotes the first four chapters to Campbell, closely dissecting his recollections and mentalité.[20] His claim that Campbell's memoir encompasses the third explanation for the relatively small decline in Knock's population must be examined further. Almost all of Campbell's recollections relate to the church, the clergy (Knock priests or Archbishop McHale) or miraculous occurrences. Almost every mention of lay parishioners relates to their interaction with the clergy. Hynes admits that Campbell does not mention the Famine directly but claims that Campbell 'alludes to hunger only once and then indirectly. Describing how the priest usually shared his breakfast after mass with the poor woman, Mary Morris'.[21] What Campbell actually says about Mary, whom he describes as a pilgrim, is:

> She was not a native of Knock but she clung to it as her home and got a living among them. In general they were a rough lot though they respected religious people. Molly Morris was also allowed the privilege of being admitted to the sacristy and always while Fr Pat [O'Grady] was having his breakfast. She managed to be on her knees behind the chair reciting the rosary, for she had beads that contained 15 decades. He might eat one or two mouthfuls of the cake that his housekeeper, Mrs McGreal, sent him and take the punch prepared by his clerk Dominic Bourke. He might also have a sip or two and then without uttering a word or looking behind him, he would first hand the cake to Molly and then the punch which many of us youngsters grudged her.[22]

Campbell does not mention famine or hunger 'but famine features in his memoir only as the occasion for the miraculous deliverance of Knock', according to Hynes.[23] Again, I believe he is inflating the evidence. The 'miraculous deliverance' referred to is about another 'holy pilgrim'. Campbell relates it thus:

A holy <u>pilgrim</u> was travelling and met a man who was driving a horse and cart and the pilgrim or holy man asked him for a ride or lift which he cheerfully granted. ... The holy pilgrim prayed and prophesied that no plague or pestilence should ever enter Knock. The writer of these lines saw the prophesy partly fulfilled, for he lived at Knock the time cholera was raging on every side of the parish, when hundreds were dying in the surrounding towns and parishes.[24]

Campbell was referring specifically to cholera, an outbreak of which occurred in the west of Ireland in the early 1830s. He cites one case only in Knock, that of Mrs Follard of Ballyhaunis.

She was a native of Knock, sister to Charles and Pat Foard of Knock. The cholera was raging in Ballyhaunis and to shun the danger [she] left Ballyhaunis ... and came to her brother's home ... but she was not many hours at Knock when she died of the cholera, but no other person took it and so the cholera ended without any more victims at Knock. So that was part of the prophecy fulfilled.[25]

In the 19th century before the causative organism of cholera, *Vibrio cholerae*, was identified and the epidemiology was determined, there were two main theories of transmission of the disease, the miasma theory and the germ theory. The miasma theory supposes that infection is spread by airborne agents from person to person whereas germ theory implies food or water-borne infection.[26] It is clear that Campbell believed the former to be the case since he remarks, 'no other person took it [cholera]'.[27] The disease is now known to be one of a contaminated water supply with the cholera vibrio spreading in drinking water contaminated with faecal material from human cholera victims. It was, in the 19th century, a disease of contaminated water tanks, pumps and pipes – in other words an urban rather than a rural problem. So, while towns like Ballyhaunis may have had raging epidemics, in rural communities like Knock, householders presumably relied on well and spring water which they did not share with many others.

Campbell mentions the diet of the people of Knock when he was living there. He comments that the inhabitants were 'not very rich, nor were they very poor.'[28] He mentions potatoes as part of the diet but there is no mention of hunger, famine, or famine fever and certainly none about post-famine population decline. The reason for the post-famine decline must be sought elsewhere. One such approach not examined in the three theories mentioned above is the differences between landlords. Hynes does suggest a detailed examination of the entire Dillon estate to see what changes in population occurred on the estate between 1841 and 1851. In the absence of such research the differences between the landlords of Knock parish is now examined.

LANDLORDS IN KNOCK PARISH

Land tenure in Knock in the second half of the 19th century was remarkably stable. The Griffith's Valuation was conducted in the area in the late 1850s and from that time, until the break-up of the estates following the Wyndham land act of 1903, there was no significant change in land ownership in the parish.[29] Prior to this valuation Lord Oranmore had an estate that included some townlands in Knock. This estate became bankrupt and was sold in 1855 under the Encumbered Estates Act.[30] The Knock townlands sold in this sale are all recorded in Griffith's with J.N. Ferrell as the 'immediate lessor', hence it is likely that he was the purchaser from Oranmore.

For the townlands of Knock parish there were five landlords recorded in Griffith's Valuation: Viscount Dillon owned 27, J.N. Ferrell 10, Francis O'Malley 4, Thomas Nowlan 2 and Francis O'Grady 1, with one townland (Churchfield) where Dillon owned most but O'Grady owned a substantial minority.[31] Excluding this last townland, the mean number of households and the mean population for each landlord's estate in the parish was calculated for the period between 1841 and 1881. The population recorded by these censuses is a function of the number of households and the mean size of household. The mean size of household for various geographical units between 1841 and 1901 (Figure 11) shows a complex result. In some areas (for example Ireland as a whole) household size declines steadily over this period, whereas for other geographical units (such as Knock parish) household size increases until 1881 and only subsequently declines. The situation is obviously quite complex and its analysis is beyond the scope of this study. For this reason, in this section, change in the size of the community will be measured by the change in the number of houses (and hence households) rather than by changes in the number of people.

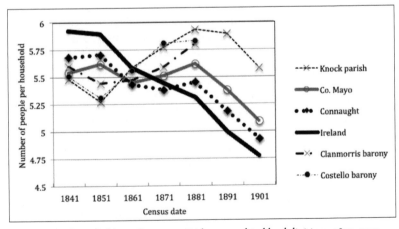

11. Mean household size for various Irish geographical land divisions, 1841–1901.
Source: Censuses of population, 1841–1901 (see Appendix 1).

The change in the number of houses on the Knock estates of the landlords is shown in Figure 12. The totals for O'Malley and O'Grady have been aggregated because of the small numbers for each individual landlord, but the trend is similar for both (see Table 2). Figure 12 demonstrates that the number of households declined on the two largest estates in the parish (Dillon and Clonbrook/Ferrall) but rose on the estates of the smaller landlords.

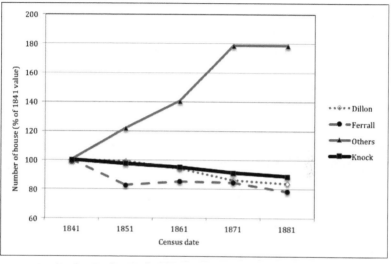

12. Changes in housing stock within Knock parish, 1841–81, by landlord.
Source: Censuses of population, 1841–1901 (see Appendix 1)

Table 2. Number of houses and people on the Knock estates of the smaller landlords, as recorded in the censuses, 1841–81

Landlord	Houses					Population				
	1841	1851	1861	1871	1881	1841	1851	1861	1871	1881
O'Grady	12	12	20	25	25	74	60	88	105	129
O'Malley	25	33	32	41	41	164	155	163	194	232
Total	37	45	52	66	66	238	215	251	299	361

Source: Censuses of population, 1821–1901 (see Appendix 1)

The declines shown on the Dillon and Farrell estates were smaller than for the rest of Co. Mayo, Connacht or the rest of Ireland, and this would support the benevolent landlord hypothesis.

OPEN AND CLOSED TOWNLANDS?

The concept of open and closed villages was developed by Mills, Holderness and others for English villages or parishes in the 19th century and earlier.[32] Mills defined closed villages as 'those controlled by either a single landowner or a small group of like-minded men who wished to keep down the level of poor rates and exert a powerful social control over the labouring classes.'[33] For open villages the gentry and clergy had less control because of 'a multiplicity of owners, many of whom had an incentive to put up cottage properties, either because they were engaged in the building trades or because their businesses stood, on balance, to gain from an influx of population'.[34] The dichotomy is generally agreed to be an oversimplification and many historians, such as Tiller, refer to an 'open' and 'closed' village spectrum.[35] Mills lists a series of characteristics which he believes typifies the open and closed village (Table 3).[36]

Table 3. Characteristics of open and closed townships or villages

Open	Closed
Large populations	Small populations
High population density	Low population density
Rapid population increase *c.*1851	Slow population increases
Many small proprietors	Large estates
Peasant families	Gentlemen's residences
Small farms	Large farms
High poor rates	Low poor rates
Rural industries and craftsmen	Little industry and few craftsmen
Shops and public houses plentiful	Few shops and public houses
Housing poor but plentiful	Housing good, but in short supply
Nonconformity common	Strong Anglican control
Radicalism and independence strong in politics and social organisation	Deference strong in politics and social organisations
Poachers	Gamekeepers

Source: Mills, *Lord and peasant*, p. 117.

Tiller pointed out that the essence of open or closed villages depended on the degree of social control exercised by the landlords. She cited the example of Castle Acre in Norfolk as 'an archetypical open community, large, uncontrolled, the nearest magistrate seven miles away, and poor but plentiful housing'.[37] The town was almost entirely owned by the Coke family of Holkham, but they 'chose not to exercise a paternalistic role in housing, education or charity'. In many areas there seems to have been a symbiotic relationship between the two types of community, with the large (open) villages supplying its surplus labour to work in nearby closed villages but without these labourers being a burden on the (poor law) ratepayers of the closed villages when work on the farms was slack. Could a similar situation have occurred in Knock? Was the tight social control (evictions, refusing to renew leases or sub-divide holdings) exercised by some landlords creating 'closed townlands'? Were other landlords allowing 'open townlands' by facilitating the construction of more housing either by sub-dividing holdings or reclamation of waste or boggy land? It would appear that in Knock this was indeed the case, and it may be true of other areas of east Mayo where the population increased after the Famine.

Between the end of the Famine in 1851 and 1881, the Dillon estate lost 64 households (17.6 per cent). The Farrell estate had a net loss of five households (5.1 per cent) over the same period. The smaller landlords gained 20 households (20.2 per cent) between them during this time, which indicates that, although there was a net loss of houses (and people) within the parish, there were some landlords who were willing and able to accommodate more families.

Were these open and closed townlands similar to the English open and closed villages? They have effectively been defined by whether they were on estates that increased or decreased in numbers of houses or people between 1851 and 1881. The top three characteristics listed by Mills (Table 3) are population size, density and change. By definition, open townlands had a greater population increase and, eventually, since townlands are a constant size, would have a higher population density, as well as a larger population, than closed townlands. Can other characteristics of English villages be identified in open and closed townlands in Ireland? Of the characteristics suggested by Mills some should be quantifiable in Irish townlands for the second half of the 19th century. It is possible to calculate the rateable value of the land and buildings within each townland in the 1850s from the Griffith's Valuation. These documents also give the acreage and the number of houses in each townland. The rateable value for land per acre could therefore be calculated as could the mean buildings rateable value per house, a proxy, perhaps, for the wealth of the population.

It is unlikely that some of the other characteristics identified by Mills, such as the presence of gamekeepers or poachers, could ever be identified systematically for Irish townlands. However, the 1901 census contains information on employment and occupation for each inhabitant so that the numbers or proportions of tradesmen could be calculated on a townland basis. For these and any other calculations, the accuracy, reliability and actual meaning of the variable is problematic, but they may be useful areas for further study.

3. Land, landlords and tenants in Knock during the 19th century

The open-field system was common throughout the British Isles from at least the Middle Ages, and probably much earlier. In Ireland it was generally known as the rundale system. Open-field systems varied both temporally and spatially, but in Ireland it consisted typically of two large fields, the infield and the outfield. These fields surrounded a settlement, which in Ireland was called a clachan. The infield, nearest to the clachan, was farmed in common in strips or small patches of land, growing principally potatoes and grain crops for food and brewing. The outfield was also farmed in common and was used for grazing cattle. Infield-outfield systems were generally confined to areas of poor soil, or in the case of north-west Ireland, poorly drained and less fertile soils.[1] Estyn Evans explains the problems of farming in 'the hilly fringes of Europe' thus:

> soils derived from barren rocks and heavily leached by excessive rains are subject to waterlogging, acidity and the accumulation of peat. Spring is the only season without excessive rain, and ploughing or digging in autumn or winter even if possible is unprofitable. Winter wheat is a risky crop in most parts, and the emphasis is on spring corn, especially oats. This meant that the arable land was free of crops from October to April, and it allowed pasturing and manuring by livestock for rather more than half the year. ... Manuring and treading of the infield by cattle and sheep were supplemented in spring by quantities of manure taken from the cabins ... In the absence of permanent fences the majority of the cattle must be moved away during the summer and those remaining carefully herded or tethered on the outfield in temporary enclosures to manure that part of the outfield which was due for cultivation.[2]

As well as the infield and outfield, each household living in the clachan had access to a small 'gort' or garden[3] as well as common meadows, bog and rough grazing.[4] Throughout the British Isles the open-field system became inefficient and was superseded by the establishment of family farms. In England and Wales this process was by means of 'enclosure', a process that could be a private and voluntary agreement between a landlord and his tenants or by an act of parliament, when enclosure could be forced through if some, or all, of the tenants objected. These parliamentary acts entailed the enclosure not just of open fields but also common grazing and waste land. They came to prominence during the second half of the 18th and the first half of the 19th century. In Ireland parliamentary acts did not occur, and thus the onus was on the landlords to initiate the change from rundale to family farming.

The inefficiency of rundale in Ireland was increased by the burgeoning population in the first half of the 19th century. It was further complicated by the fact that the cottiers and small farmers were cultivating smaller and smaller infield plots and thus becoming reliant on the potato for their subsistence. Lord George Hill gives an example of the situation in Donegal just before the Famine:

> In some instances a tenant having any part of a townland (no matter how small), had his proportion in thirty or forty different places, and without fences between them. One poor man who had his inheritance in thirty-two different places, abandoned them in utter despair of ever being able to make them out … In one instance a small field of half an acre was held by twenty-six people.[5]

Another example comes from Co. Mayo, in the 20th century. The clachan of Rathlacken consisted, in 1918, of 56 families occupying 1,500 scattered plots:

> some of them no more than a dozen square yards in area. A two-acre holding was split into eighteen tiny plots, and on the average twenty-seven lots were held by each farm. Such was the confusion that it was not until 1942 that the process of redistribution and consolidation of holdings was completed.[6]

It is apparent therefore that the rundale system encouraged two trends in Irish land management, namely, sub-division of plots and 'perpetual squabbling and fighting.'[7]

RUNDALE IN KNOCK PARISH (DURING THE 19TH CENTURY)

Rundale survived well into the 19th century. Evidence from the Devon Commission to the parliament in Westminster claimed that 58 per cent of land in Co. Mayo was farmed under the rundale system (in 1845).[8] Evidence for the situation in Knock parish comes from several sources. Bald's map (surveyed in 1809–17) shows several clachans in or near the parish, including one in Carrowmore townland (Figure 13). By 1836, when the Tithe Applotment books were compiled, a large proportion of the tithe payers were listed with the words 'and partners' to their names indicating that the land was farmed communally, presumably in a rundale system.

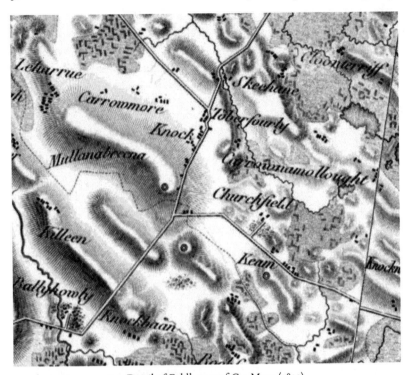

13. Detail of Bald's map of Co. Mayo (1830).
Source: *A map of the Maritime County of Mayo in 25 sheets commenced in 1809 and terminated in 1817*
by William Bald F.R.S.E., printed in 1830 (Mayo County Library, viewed online at:
http://www.mayolibrary on 9 June 2020)

There is also direct evidence about the survival of rundale on the estates of
the two largest landlords in Knock, John Nolan Ferrall and Viscount Dillon.
Ferrall purchased the 1753-acre Rockfield estate in Knock parish in 1855 from
the encumbered estate of Lord Oranmore and Brown.[9] In the same year he
purchased the nearby Logboy estate of his bankrupt uncle, Edmund Nolan.
The Logboy estate consisted of nine townlands amounting to 1,395 acres in the
neighbouring parish of Annagh, and had been 'under the control of chancery'
since 1845.[10] There is no direct evidence that the Rockfield estate was farmed
in rundale at this time, but the Logboy estate was assumed to have been farmed
under such a system.[11]

For Viscount Dillon the evidence is clear. Writing specifically about Dillon's
Irish estate, Coulter observed in 1862:

> The rundale system existed here, as in other properties in Mayo, and
> led to that minute subdivision of holdings which has been found to be
> productive of so many mischievous effects. The striping of the lands was

commenced systematically in 1840, and has been carried out over at least two-thirds of the estate; and wherever the old system still remains, it is owing to the existence of old leases.[12]

It seems possible that the maps of the Dillon estate were drawn up at the time that rundale ended and the farms were 'squared off'. There are 85 Dillon maps, which are now in the National Library of Ireland, that are dateable.[13] Their dates range from the 1840s to the 1870s and thus the hypothesis that their production corresponded to the end of rundale within the townland or townlands mapped, can be compared to Coulter's estimate of the timing of the demise of rundale on the Dillon estate. The dates of the maps are plotted graphically in Figure 14. The modal date of the maps is 1855–9 which is consistent with Coulter's statement. Indeed 72 of the maps (84.7%) date to before 1862 when Coulter's estimate of two-thirds (67%) was made, suggesting a somewhat faster demise than Coulter was indicating.

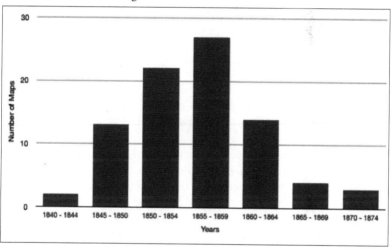

14. Dates of the Dillon estate maps.
Source: Maps of the estate of Viscount Dillon, vols 1–3 (NLI, 16 M 4–6)

Landlords were keen to eradicate rundale. For example in Co. Donegal, Lord George Hill writing about his 23,000-acre Gweedore estate maintained that:

> The rundale system was a complete bar to any attempt at improvement; as, on a certain day, all the cattle belonging to the townland were brought from the mountains and allowed to run indiscriminately over the arable land. And in spring no individual occupier would set or sow, or labour in the fields, before a certain day, when the cattle were again sent to the hills, until after harvest.[14]

On Lord Dillon's estate:

> The land was in rundale and wilderness; very small and only scattered patches were reclaimed. The small plots belonging to different small occupiers were scattered in the most indiscriminate manner. Each man had a piece reclaimed near his cabin, at some distance a plot of bottom land, and elsewhere a tract of bog. There were neither roads fences or drains.
>
> ... Mr Strickland had the land surveyed, and each man's claim specially recorded; the site and condition of his house were carefully noted. Several houses had generally been placed together in small clusters. The area held by each occupier, the proportion of cultivated and bog, and its value, were carefully ascertained. In laying out the new divisions or small farms each occupier was given as nearly as possible the same quantity he held before, but all in one piece, including part of each quality of land – arable, bottom, reclaimed, and bog or waste – and each new farm or holding was valued and charged its own separate rent. Hundreds of little farms proportioned to the claims of the occupiers were thus symmetrically mapped out in stripes and carefully examined by Mr Strickland. The man whose house was left standing was usually allowed to retain possession of it and take the farm on which it stood. If from one of his neighbours he had acquired a portion of reclaimed land, he would have to pay for it. The older cabins were pulled down and rebuilt on the fitting situation, assisted by the landlord. The wholesale redistribution and striping of the land is not such a seriously expensive affair; it required, however, much time and trouble, with no little tact and judgment, to balance rival claims and assess how much had to be credited for disseverance of a piece of good land, or what was to be debited for the new or improved house. Rent with entry charges and rebates being duly arranged by Mr Strickland, the new holdings were allotted, and the keen little farmers, most jealous regarding their interests and rights, unanimously proclaim the great pains and labour bestowed on these troublesome little awards, as well as the justice with which they have been made.[15]

This, no doubt, was how 'reforming' landlords viewed their programmes of modernization. What is not recorded in contemporaneous documents is what the tenants thought about such 'improvements'. We can, however, get some idea of what the tenants thought of it all from their reaction to the process. It seems that they were reluctant to submit to, if not downright hostile to, such changes, since most contemporary accounts indicate that the rundale system ended when the leases 'fell in'. If the tenantry had been enthusiastic about the new system they would surely have surrendered their leases at the earliest opportunity.

Coulter does state that 'the people are fully alive to the benefit of having their lands properly divided, and in some instances they have voluntarily surrendered their leases for the purpose of having this effected'.[16] The relevant phrase here is surely 'in some instances'. It implies that the remainder of the tenantry did not voluntarily surrender leases. Finlay Dun was another commentator who wrote about the Dillon estate, nearly 20 years after Coulter's account. Both men gave highly favourable accounts of the management of the estate and both praise the land steward, Charles Strickland, praise which borders on sycophancy at times. Dun goes further than Coulter when he claims that Strickland striped the land 'as the old leases expired'.[17] Both gentlemen imply that the tenants of the Dillon estate were largely hostile to the changes Strickland was introducing.

If the advantages to the tenants were as good as the landlords maintained why were the tenants hostile to these changes? Was it the demise of the clachan? In Gweedore, Lord George Hill noted that 'the pleasure the people feel in assembling and chatting together, made them consider the removal of the houses, from the [clachans] to the separate farms, a great grievance.'[18] William Wilde (father of Oscar), writing in 1853, commented on the sociability of such communal living which included the mutual help available in times of sickness and of 'sympathy in joy and sorrow, [and] of combined operations of defence against bailiff and gauger.'[19] Estyn Evans elaborated on the benefits of the clachans:

> There were ceilidhes and spinning parties, and many a clachan had a shanachie (story-teller) and its fiddler or piper … who accompanied with folk-tunes. Folk-songs, occupational airs and legendary tales were kept alive in this way. Apart from the co-operation implicit in the openfield system there was a good deal of sharing in other ways.[20]

One of these other ways may have been the dissemination of news. By the middle of the 19th century, regional and local newspapers were starting to be published throughout the country, and with literacy rising (see Figure 5) 'The clachan housing system … provided a ready audience for a newspaper story if there was even one person in the community who could read.'[21] If this was indeed the case the audience would have learned of other reasons to be wary of such changes.

In 1846, at Ballinlass on the Gerard estate in Co. Galway, 61 families, consisting of 270 people, were evicted to facilitate the landlord's plan for a grazing farm.[22] The 'clearances' generated much press coverage at the time and may well have influenced clachan-based tenants, both at Knock and throughout Ireland, to be wary of any landlord-based schemes. It is also possible that rack-renting may have been a concern to the tenantry. The work of modern historians such as Vaughan and Solow has largely 'discredited the traditional nationalist image of the rapacious, rack-renting post-Famine landlord.'[23] The work of Jordan has concluded that 'the majority of Mayo landlords appear to have been content with regularly remitted low to moderate rents.'[24] There were exceptions, however. Two Mayo landlords that have been accused of raising rents excessively, between the time of the Famine and the land war, were the marquis of Sligo and the earl of Lucan. Lord Sligo claimed in 1881 that he had written off rent arrears during the Famine and had (temporarily) lowered the rents of his tenants. Rents were subsequently raised gradually to levels he believed to be 'fair and moderate'.[25] In other words, he claimed that all he was doing was catching up. His tenants did not see it that way. 'Patrick M'Ginn, a tenant of Lord Sligo in the townland of Arderry, told the [Bessborough] commissioners that between 1853 and 1869 his rent had been raised three times from £28 to £98.'[26] Possibly other Mayo tenants were scared the same would happen to them.

If landlords wanted land reform, and tenants were reluctant to change their housing, there is no explanation as to why the landlords did not just reform the land allocation while retaining the clachans. Notwithstanding the motives of both landlords and tenants, the transformation from rundale to family farms undeniably took place. What effect the reform of rundale and the demise of the clachans had on the levels of communal violence in the second half of the 19th century will be discussed in the next section.

Many commentators have claimed that the clachan housing system strengthened kinship ties between families but also generated violence both within and between the communities. Kelly, for example, noted that 'The neighbours in a clachan, who often had ties of kinship, co-operated with one another in farming tasks such as harvesting ... [but] the cohesion within the clachans ... was often matched by rivalry between them, finding expression in faction fights on fair days and other occasions of public assembly.'[27] He also cites the example of Tulrahan, a townland on the Logboy estate less than ten miles from Knock, which was notorious for its faction fights during annual pattern day celebrations.[28] Estyn Evans summed up:

> with the close kinship bonds went the corresponding rivalries with adjacent neighbourhoods ... these rivalries broke out characteristically into feuds and blood-letting at fairs and gatherings. But in later days, at any rate, internal rivalries and squabbles were more conspicuous and found more opportunities within overgrown kinship groups which had become too complicated to function smoothly.[29]

VIOLENCE IN 19TH-CENTURY KNOCK

Daniel Campbell, in his history of Knock, provides evidence that Knock shared with its neighbours a legacy of communal and interpersonal violence and protest. On the very first page of his account he mentions the patron saint of the parish, Saint John the Baptist, whose pattern day is 24 June. On that day Campbell claims he had 'seen many cut heads and bleeding noses on the occasion: it was the only day at Knock for a spree.'[30] He also mentions that factions existed in Knock during his childhood (he was born in 1825). He names the Flatley family as leaders of one faction. Michael Flatley, of Wingfield, Knock, was a convert to Protestantism who became involved in a dispute with the parish priest. According to Campbell, 'he called the priest everything but a gentleman. He ... called all his friends and relations to assist him for they were the strongest faction in the parish. Strange to say they did rally round their kinsman and did their best to ... execute his threats.'[31] Campbell names another faction in the parish, led by the Corrie and Byrne families, who sided with the priest.[32] It is not entirely clear whether Campbell is referring to two groups who represented different sides in a specific dispute, or whether they were factions on a permanent or semi-permanent basis. On another occasion, a Flatley family member (there were several Flatley families in the parish) tendered, unsuccessfully, for repair work on the chapel. 'This stirred up the old flame and the Flatleys once more were not the best friends of the priests.'[33] The fact that Campbell documents two separate disputes both involving Flatley family members suggests that, in pre-Famine Knock, factions were part-and-parcel of parish life.

Newspapers of the period support this interpretation. In July 1834 it was reported in the local press that an ass belonging to John Flattly (sic) of Knock had his ears cut off. The report concludes 'Flattly has of late been much persecuted by some of the inhabitants of Knock, and his wife threatened, in consequence of (as he states) having changed his religion and become a Protestant.'[34] This obviously refers to the same feud as reported by Campbell.

The Flatleys were not always the victims. On Christmas day 1837 James Jeffers was badly beaten after attending mass at the chapel at Knock. This incident highlights the problems associated with the nature of violence in 19th-century Ireland. Was this a faction fight? If so, what was the fighting about? Thuente has concluded that 'faction-fighting was essentially an immensely popular and violent pastime'.[35] The attack on Jeffers suggests a more complex situation, at least in this instance. The events of that night are convoluted, resulting in a petty session civil case, and three criminal trials, occurring over a period of several years, with motives hinted at, but not specifically mentioned. Those accused of the attack produced defences including mistaken identity and perjury by prosecution witnesses, and to make matters more confusing, the accounts that have come down to us have been filtered through fragmentary and possibly inaccurate reporting by the press.

The undisputed facts of the case(s) are that Jeffers attended the third mass in Knock chapel on Christmas day 1837.[36] After mass he went with his wife and mother to a nearby shebeen where they drank some whiskey. After leaving the shebeen, a fight occurred during which Jeffers was beaten, with 'sticks and stones', by four men. Jeffers suffered a broken skull and even by 1840 was 'not well yet' according to his wife.

The whole judicial process for this crime was a protracted affair. The first trial occurred on 24 July 1840. John Flatley was indicted for the malicious assault of James Jeffers. During this trial it transpired that Jeffers had 'processed the prisoner [Flatley] to the sessions for compensation for the injury, and the process was dismissed.'[37] Flatley was found guilty by the jury who 'recommended him to mercy.'[38] The second trial was on Friday 6 August 1841, nearly five years after the attack happened. The report in the *Mayo Constitution* was short and to the point. In its entirety it reads: 'John Prendergast was indicted for assaulting Thomas (sic) Jeffers on Christmas Day, returning from mass. The parties had been drinking in a shebeen house at the chapel, and a fight commenced, in the course of which several persons received a severe beating. The prisoner was sentenced to 18 months imprisonment.'[39] The third trial did not occur until March 1843. The accused was John Bourke, the son of Dominick Bourke, the parish clerk. As with the Flatley case the jury found him guilty but recommended mercy. When asked by the judge on what grounds they had made this recommendation, the foreman said it was 'on account of his good character' to which the judge replied, 'good character is no justification for breaking a man's skull.'[40] Prendergast, having by then served his sentence, was a defence witness in this trial. He admitted to having taken part in one of the two fights that occurred that night but denied that Bourke was there. The motive for the attack on Jeffers remains unclear. It seems that some sort of faction fight took place that Christmas night but was it just a recreational pastime as Thuente maintains, or were other motives involved? Jeffers is reported to have said at Bourke's trial that at mass he 'gave his Reverence some money, perhaps those who beat him gave none.'[41] Could Jeffers have been attacked because he paid the priest's Christmas dues?

In 1836, the year before Jeffers was attacked, the *Mayo Constitution*, a conservative paper in both senses, reported considerable lawlessness in Costello barony, associated with 'Captain Rock' and the rockite agitation. On 5 March of that year, a large number of men from Aughamore

> traversed the parish of Knock, administering oaths to the inhabitants, binding them to refuse the payment of tithes ... Owning to a dispute among the people with respect to a favourite Priest, one party being anxious for his removal, and the other party for retaining him in the parish, the Rockites also swore several of the inhabitants of the same parish against paying their Parish Priest his dues, or to have their children baptized by him.[42]

Daniel Campbell, in his history of the parish, recalls this, or a remarkably similar, episode:

I remember some parties stricking against the priest's salary and wanted to reduce him 2*d*. per year and give him 2/- instead of 2/2. I do not know who began it, but I know that it was got up at Aughamore and a procession was formed and it was getting larger as they marched from house to house and extorted a promise from the owner of the house to pay no more than 2/- per year, but did not interfere with the collection at the church on Easter or Christmas day. They were not satisfied with the promise above mentioned, for each house had to send one with the procession until they went to a certain number of houses. I forget how many. But I though a boy, which I am sorry to say had to go for fear's sake, for my father would not go on any account on such an errand. And for fear of doing us an injury, I was advised to go instead of my father. It had the desired effect and instead of the half yearly 1/1 it was 1/- for the whole family, not amounting to ½*d*. per week … The church was free except on Christmas Day and Easter Sunday, and on those days there was a collection at the eastern door.[43]

Two other instances of apparent faction fights at Knock have been identified in the press. On 31 May 1835 Edmund Mellee (or Melbee) died sixteen days after a 'cake' at the chapel of Knock when several people were alleged to have been fighting. Michael Morelly was indicted for his murder but was convicted of manslaughter.[44] On the eve of the Famine in February 1845 an instance of 'the old system of club-law and profanation of the sabbath' occurred at Knock, again at the chapel. A 'lawless multitude' of over 400 armed men from the nearby parish of Kilcolman surrounded the chapel during mass. The motive, as stated in the press, was 'to revenge a party spleen'. Perhaps it is a co-incidence that 'one poor fellow named Flatley was beaten most dreadfully.'[45] Following the Famine, press reports of fighting at Knock seem to have ceased.

For the families that had managed to survive the Famine and the wave of evictions that followed in the early 1850s, life gradually improved in the following decades. 'The widespread adoption of livestock raising following the Famine had not created an integrated society in Co. Mayo … Rather, it altered the structure of, but did not diminish a long-standing division in the county between a progressive economic elite … and the rural poor'.[46] During the 1860s and 1870s a coalition of merchants, tradesmen and substantial farmers, largely Catholic and nationalist in outlook, began to exert political influence, partly through pressure in parliament but also through election to, and influence upon, the local government system in Ireland at that time – the poor law board of guardians. From the late 1860s a more militant strain of nationalism, the Fenians, together with agrarian radicals, whose aims were to achieve reform or abolition of landlordism in Ireland, was added to the mix.[47]

There was a harvest failure in 1877, with only a partial recovery the following year, so the 1879 harvest, throughout Ireland, was crucial, but as Roy Foster has explained:

Potato yields suffered particularly; blight reappeared in the south-west. Freak rain and cold throughout the summer and another hopeless harvest were accompanied by a drastic fuel shortage in the west. This coincided with falling prices brought about by the entry of American grain, and even beef, on to the British market. ... Potato production had fallen by three-quarters, and starvation loomed in the west, where significantly, earnings from migrant labour also plummeted disastrously because of contemporary recession in Britain.[48]

This agricultural crisis combined, as it was, with political agitation led not to violence, but to peaceful protest in what became known as the land war.

'THREE CHEERS FOR THE ZULUS': THE AGRICULTURAL CRISIS AND THE LAND WAR IN
KNOCK, 1879

The agricultural crisis in the late 1870s hit Mayo hard. The Dublin Mansion House Committee for Relief and Distress in Ireland sent one of its members, J.A. Fox, to report on conditions in Mayo. His report makes for sobering reading.[49] Writing from Mayo in 1880, he warned the committee that it was his painful duty 'to report, on unimpeachable authority, that many thousands of human beings would have died of starvation during the last few months except for the relief by various charity committees'.[50] He describes the conditions that he found in 'some' of the hovels:

The children are nearly naked. Bedding there is none, everything of that kind having long since gone to the pawn-office, as proved to me by numerous tickets placed in my hands for inspection in well-nigh every hovel. A layer of old straw covered by the dirty sacks which conveyed the seed potatoes and artificial manure in the spring is the sole provision of thousands – with this exception, that little babies in wooden boxes are occasionally indulged with a bit of old flannel stitched onto the sacking. Sometimes even charity itself had failed, and the mother of the tender young family was found absent, begging for the loan of some Indian meal from other recipients of charitable relief – the father being, in almost every instance, away in England labouring to make out some provision for the coming winter.[51]

The situation in Knock and surrounding districts seems not to have been quite as bad, for, later in his report, Fox states: 'There has been destitution and privation in the neighbourhood of Ballyhaunis, Knock, and Claremorris, as elsewhere, but the squalor and misery are not so widespread as in the Swinford district'.[52]

When it comes to explaining how such a situation arose, opinions differed. The Royal Irish Constabulary sent a circular to their district sub-inspectors in December 1879 asking them to state the probable cause for the crop failures that year. The reply from the Claremorris district reads, 'The bad yields of the crops in this district, particularly the potato crop, is entirely owing to the wetness of the season'.[53] Whilst this was undoubtedly the cause of the crop failures, another reason for the miserable state of the tenantry in Mayo is suggested by Fox:

> It is no more than stating a fact, provocative of no controversy, to add, that the residual gentry of Mayo have now, as was the case in 1847–8 not only no sympathy with the absentee landlords, but that they would on the contrary, and for obvious reasons, gladly see the system of absenteeism discouraged by the heaviest penalties practicable.[54]

The agricultural crisis does seem to have been the catalyst for significant change in the attitude of the Mayo smallholders. They seemed to have lost faith in the prevailing system and were responsive to change.[55] Three disparate groups within the county coalesced to form an uneasy coalition in an attempt to bring about reform. These groups were the Tenants' Defence Association (TDA), the Irish Parliamentary Party (IPP) and the Fenians. The TDA was an organization whose principal aims were to protect the tenantry from rack-renting and eviction. It was largely run by large farmers and graziers and had little representation in the west of Ireland. In May 1876 the Ballinasloe Tenants' Association was set up in Co. Galway. This association was enthusiastically supported by the *Connaught Telegraph* newspaper which, under the auspices of its editor and proprietor, James Daly, also encouraged the establishment of a Co. Mayo branch of the TDA. Daly, together with John Louden, a Westport barrister, eventually succeeded, and in Castlebar on 26 October 1878 a committee was established. Daly and Louden, who were both also large-scale graziers, persuaded the Irish Parliamentary Party MP for Mayo, John O'Connor Power, to speak at this meeting and rally the whole party to the cause. Power was on the Supreme Council of the IRB when he became an MP in 1874 and, although his militancy had diminished in the intervening years, he was happy to share the platform with them in what was known as the 'New Departure' of unofficial cooperation between Fenians and constitutional nationalists.[56] The first meeting organized by the TDA was held at Irishtown in Co. Mayo, just a few miles distant from Knock. This is widely recognized as the start of the Irish Land War.[57]

The organization of this meeting was undertaken by Daly and Michael Davitt, a Fenian who had recently been released from prison. The choice of Irishtown as the venue was apparently due to discontent among the tenantry on the Bourke estate in the townland of Quinaltagh, just over the county border in

Co. Galway. This discontent was due to rent increases and threats of eviction. Details are confused and conflicting, especially over the role played by the Revd Geoffrey Canon Burke, the brother of the landlord.[58] Suffice to say, the clergy in general were notable by their absence, so that 'in the absence of parish priests to organize and lead them, the crowd that marched to the meeting was arranged into contingents and led to prearranged places by local Fenians'.[59] The crowd was estimated as between 7,000 and 13,000 who cheered enthusiastically the speeches of Daly, Louden, and O'Connor Power as well as Matthew Harris from the Supreme Council of the IRB.[60]

In the same issue of the *Connaught Telegraph* that reported the Irishtown meeting, a further tenants' defence meeting was announced for Westport in early June 1879 with the aim of 'giving expression to their [the tenant farmers'] grievances and of demanding an immediate reduction of rents'.[61] Before this meeting occurred two other meetings were held in south-east Mayo, apparently organized by the Fenians, without the support of Daly and his newspaper. The first of these was held in Claremorris on 25 May 1879. It was organized by two Claremorris shopkeepers, John O'Keane and P.J. Gordan. Gordan was suspected of being a Fenian and O'Keane was said to be their District Master. Both were subsequently on the police list of persons whose arrest was recommended under the protection of property and persons act, 1881.[62] Both were also known to Archdeacon Cavanagh, the parish priest of Knock.[63] The gathering attracted a crowd of 2,000 who marched through the town to the meeting which was held in a field near to the Workhouse.[64] Unlike the Irishtown meeting report in the *Connaught Telegraph*, which was extensive, the papers coverage of the Claremorris meeting amounted to just a couple of column inches. This may be because of Daly's distaste for physical-force nationalism, but another possible reason could be due to the demands of the protestors.[65] They passed a resolution, by acclamation, 'calling on landlords to give the lands at present occupied by graziers to small farmers at fair rents.'[66] Daly was, after all, a newspaper proprietor *and* a large grazier!

On the same page that reported the Claremorris meeting, the *Telegraph* ran an item in its 'Local Notes' column. It read:

> The Revd B. Kavanagh, PP, on Sunday last addressed his congregation at the chapel of Knock, denouncing nationalists. The address has caused great indignation amongst his parishioners, and it is rumoured that the Revd Gentleman will hear further on the subject. These denunciations will affect no good, as Father Kavanagh will, very probably, learn in due course.[67]

Father Cavanagh did hear more on the subject and he did not have to wait very long for a reply. The Fenians arranged a second meeting for the following Sunday (1 June) which must have sent tensions soaring, for, just a week after his sermon, Father Cavanagh witnessed thousands of demonstrators descending on his parish. The *Connaught Telegraph* reported in its next issue:

> Monster Indignation Meeting at Knock
> One of the largest and most imposing demonstrations that has ever taken place in this part of the country ... was held at Knock, ... on Sunday the 1st of June. Fully fifteen thousand men marched with military precision ... to the place of meeting, so that when all were assembled there could not have been less than from twenty to thirty thousand present ... What brought this vast multitude together, in a measure, without notice or advertisement? Well, happlly, (sic) an unusual occurrence. It was to enter a solemn and emphatic protest against the language used by the Venerable Archdeacon Kavanagh from the altar of the Parish Church on the previous Sunday. As we are all aware, the Tenant farmers have been endeavouring for some time past to impress on their landlords that owing to the present depression, and the falling off in the value of all agricultural produce, it is essentially necessary to the well-being of both classes that a reduction of the present exorbitant rents should take place.

The article went on to say that the tenant farmers of Knock, Aughamore, Barnacarroll, Kilvine, Annagh, and the surrounding district, organized the protest to press home their demands. They accused the archdeacon of attempting to suppress the meeting 'for the purpose of shielding certain landlords who were not inclined to accede to the just and reasonable demands.' The priest was said to have accused the organizers of

> sinister and ulterior motives, and personally accused Mr J. O'Keane, of Claremorris, to be engaged with others in preparing the country for a revolution. The people, when they heard these gross misrepresentations coming from a quarter they least expected, resolved upon entering an emphatic protest against them as being malicious in the highest degree. Hence the great demonstration of last Sunday.[68]

The paper continued to describe the speech made by the chairman, Mr Tobias Merrick, a 'respectable tenant-farmer' who spoke of his 'pain and sorrow' at having to hold such a meeting and he 'hoped the day would never come that priests and people would be found in opposite camps, but if such occurs it will not be the people's fault.' He added that he 'would be very sorry to say anything disrespectful to a Roman Catholic clergyman: but this much he would say, don't stand between the people and their rights; if you do, you must be prepared to accept the consequences.' The article mentioned that there were other speakers but did not go into any detail. Fortunately for posterity, there were others who noted what was said by the other speakers. The police were monitoring the meeting and their report was sent to Dublin Castle a couple of days later, by Inspector H. Carter. His report concentrated on these other speakers – the Fenians, who included O'Keane and Gordan. This report, if accurate, gives a taste of the militant flavour of the occasion:

> Meeting at Knock, County of Mayo
> Claremorris 3rd June 1879
>
> All the men, about 300 who <u>marched</u> to Knock on that day, assembled at a place called Baring-Carroll and proceeded thence in fours.
>
> They were profusely decorated with green sashes, rosettes, ribbons and laurel branches and leaves. They were commanded by J.W. Nally, suspect, Balla, John O'Kane, suspect, of this town, and P.J. Gordon, bootmaker, who lives here also. Another man who was introduced as a Mr Jones of Dublin had a command, but he was actually a person called Sheridan, who ~~was~~ is a native of Bohold in this district. All these men addressed the people assembled on the occasion who numbered about 1500; Sheridan was the first who delivered a speech. He said "Father Cavanagh (PP) had endeavoured to stamp them as blackguards, he had done everything to brand them (cries down with him – off his supplies.) He should not trample on the people who hoped to benefit their Country. He had referred to one man by name (Shame, and nine cheers for O'Kane) and said that he was actually drawing money and purchasing arms – The only motive is the common benefit of our Country, that, by banding themselves together against the tyrant Landlords. There were police present : let them hear a sample of their ideas. Let them openly declare their determination to stand and die together. They were threatened with settlers (the Constabulary in allusion to the formation of a barrack at Knock) but they should be no longer luke warm or cowardly, but proclaim in daylight what was required. &c.

The report also summarizes O'Kane's speech. He is said to have repudiated the 'wanton attack upon him' maintaining that he only wanted Irish freedom. According to the report, O'Kane continued:

> It was said they were fenians – If that means haters of British Rule they were all fenians. Did Father Cavanagh wish to be reconciled to British Rule? Who made their country a desert? Would they be reconciled? (three cheers for the Zulus) They should wait for their opportunity. England was so hostile as of old. The fair fields of Ireland are converted into bullock pastures. He had promises from America – If they work together they would work out the freedom of their Country. When England would be engaged by Russia it would then be their time. He did not want to conceal that when the opportunity offered it would be embraced.

No police station was required at Knock : It would be an outrage to bring those ruffians – the police – amongst the people, It would not deter them to do their duty. They would resist the invaders and drive them into the Atlantic. His time was called and he'd not depart from it. Gordon directed the people to pay no rent without getting an abatement. If the landlords resisted they'd make the tenants not pay.

A Resolution was then put forward by Sheridan in which was proposed that Nolan Farrell's Tenants (in this district) should hold out against their tyrant landlord, the scoundrel who would crowd the workhouses of their saxon enemies and their Gaols & that they should stand together &c. ...

(Sd) H Carter.[69]

In his biography of Cavanagh, Ua Cadhain claimed (without stating his source) that in 1879, because the archdeacon was preaching caution and restraint –

at a special secret meeting ... [of Fenians] the subject [of what to do with Archdeacon Cavanagh] was fully discussed. Various suggestions were offered, but rejected. The extreme penalty was considered fitting to meet the menace of a dangerous priest who talked of the moral law, a man who warned his people about the danger of taking direction from unknown leaders ... At length it was resolved that a lesser punishment than death would meet the position in the district. It would probably be sufficient warning to other parishes, especially when the 'heads' had reached the conclusion that milder punishments were, at this stage, the correct procedure.[70]

According to Ua Cathain, the punishment decided upon was to issue a series of threats and 'finally to have his ears cut off.'[71] A date and a perpetrator were decided upon but before the mutilation could be carried out, the Knock apparition occurred on 21 August and this seems to have resulted in a sea-change in the local atmosphere. Ua Cathain, again without citing sources, maintains that the local militants who knew of the plot, 'called together their friends in the parish and proclaimed they would rally round the pastor, regardless of consequences to themselves, and challenge any man to touch him'.[72] Whether such a plot ever existed or whether it was just part of the Cavanagh hagiography may never be known. Other historians such as Paul Bew have cast doubt on this story, pointing out that 'direct assassination of landlords, agents or peasantry who failed to support the popular will were frequent occurrences, but in no instance was a Catholic priest done to death in this fashion'.[73] Whatever the case feelings and tensions were certainly running high in the summer of 1879.

Just a couple of months later an apparition was reported at Knock, news of which was to reverberate around the world and point the spotlight on this little Co. Mayo village again. At the end of October of that year Father Cavanagh began to keep a diary entitled 'An account of the Miraculous Cures wrought at the gable of the chapel here, where the Blessed Virgin Mary, the Immaculate Mother, appeared, on the night of the 21st of August last'. The very first item, in his list of over one hundred, was as follows:

> 1. Delia Gordon, daughter of Mr P.J. Gordon, of Claremorris; deafness and pain in the left ear. This, the first cure reported, was instantaneous. It occurred on Sunday, the 31st August. Full particulars ... [were] ... related to me by Mr and Mrs P.J. Gordon ... The cure was effected by putting into the ear a small particle of cement.[74]

Conclusion

'There is a history in all men's lives'

William Shakespeare[1]

Most studies of the 'land war', a period of rural agitation throughout Ireland, that started in the late 1870s, have concentrated on the national picture. Even the more localized histories that have been published have been conducted at the county level.[2] The primary aim of this study is to investigate the tensions that existed within a rural community at this time, at the parish or even the townland level, using the parish of Knock, Co. Mayo as the example.

Data contained within the 1901 census, the first extant Irish census to include information on individual families, contains a wealth of other information that can be analysed to illuminate aspects of 19th-century Irish life at the parish or even townland level. The first chapter has highlighted some of these for the people of 19th-century Knock. The concept of age is one example. There is evidence that age was a far less precise concept in the 19th century than it is today. Since the 1911 census was conducted precisely 10 years and two days after the 1901 census, one would expect that, if everybody was recording their age accurately, everyone would have a recorded age that differed by 10 years between the two censuses. This was not the case, however. It can be seen from Figure 2 that many people (and not just the eldest within the community), were rounding up their ages to the nearest ten-years. Comparison of the two censuses could also be used to identify families that had lost children and named subsequent children after their dead siblings.

The 1901 census can also illuminate questions relating to literacy within the Knock population. If one assumes that the vast majority of respondents in the census who were literate had learnt to read and write as children, and that migration in and out of the parish was small, then literacy within the parish was almost 50 per cent in the 1820s and remained at that level until after the Famine. From that time it rose until, by the 1880s, almost everybody over the age of 11 was literate. Other census questions can be used to learn about the population at parish or townland level, that of the Irish language, for example. It is postulated that for bilingual respondents within the parish, their primary and secondary languages could be identified. If this is indeed the case then, at Knock until the 1870s, only a small minority of inhabitants (less than 20 per cent) had English as their first language, but for those born after that date the proportion rose steeply, so that by the 20th century almost all the population spoke English as their mother tongue. Household structure is another topic that can be studied from data recorded in the census. In 1901 43 per cent of families were nuclear households, that is consisting of husband, wife and children only. It would seem that the vast majority of households within the parish contained nuclear families throughout most of their existence. This is because it appears that most of the households that were not nuclear households in 1901 (by the strict definition of the term) were either about to become nuclear households or else had previously been nuclear. Those that were about to become nuclear households consisted of newly married couples who had yet to have children. Households that seemed to have previously contained nuclear families included those where one parent was missing, either dead or staying elsewhere on census night, and also older couples living alone after all their children had left home. Examples of multigenerational households containing non-relatives (servants, employees, boarders etc.) or more distant relatives (nephews and nieces, cousins, siblings, parents, grandchildren etc.) were rare in Knock in 1901.

The second chapter examined the population changes within the parish between 1821 and 1901, which showed the same trend as Ireland as a whole. That is, the population rose until the time of the Famine, when it declined steeply and continued to decline for the rest of the century. The rate of decline, in percentage terms, was slower for Knock parish than the county (Mayo), province (Connacht) or the national rate (see Figure 10). In a rural community, such as Knock, where the vast majority of people made their living from the land, the number of households on that land is as important as the number of people on the land. The income of landlords, for example, depends on the number of households paying their rent, not the number of people present on his land. If the household size remains constant for any period under study, percentage changes for households and people should be identical. But, as is demonstrated in Figure 11, changes in household size varied across the country between 1841 and 1901. For Ireland as a whole, household size fell every decade over this period but in Knock parish (likewise Costello barony) household size fell between 1841 and 1851 and then rose steadily until 1881, before falling again.

Knock parish is situated within two of Mayo's baronies – Clanmorris and Costello. Population data for baronies was not collated after the 1881 census, but up until then the two baronies had noticeably different rates of post-Famine decline. The population of Costello barony declined by only about 5 per cent between 1841 and 1881 whereas the decline in Clanmorris was about 35 per cent. Others have commented on the variation of post-Famine population changes in eastern Mayo. Cousens has suggested that the parts of the county that experienced small decreases, or even increases in population following the Famine, were areas with large amounts of unclaimed wastelands that could be reclaimed for smallholders to occupy.[3] In this study, it is suggested that landlords' policy towards their tenants was an important determining factor in the post-Famine decline. In Knock parish this certainly appears to be the case. The two largest landlords in the parish, Viscount Dillon and J.N. Ferrall, both saw the number of households decline by over 20 per cent in that part of their estates in Knock parish. For the other, smaller, landlords in the parish, the number of households actually rose between 1841 and 1901 (Figure 12). This could suggest that these landlords, with smaller estates who lived locally, may have had a more sympathetic (or laissez-faire) attitude towards the sub-division of land. Figure 12 also shows that the decline in households on the Ferrall estate occurred largely between 1841 and 1851 and remained largely static thereafter, whereas on the Dillon estate the decline occurred throughout the second half of the 19th century.

The reputation of these two landlords is radically different. Although Lord Dillon was an absentee landlord, his reputation, largely due to his estate manager, George Strickland, was good. Both in print and in the press they were praised as model landlord and agent. Ferrall, on the other hand, was subject to hostility from his tenants and negative comments in the press. It remains a possibility that both had the same aims – to reduce the number of tenants on their estate but by different means; Dillon with the support, or acquiescence, of his tenantry; Ferrall despite the opposition of his.

Also considered in the second chapter is the concept of 'open' and 'closed' townlands, a concept that is the Irish equivalent of English open and closed villages. From the evidence of the townlands of the parish of Knock, it would appear that open and closed townlands did exist, at least in terms of population change. Whether open and closed townlands differ in the other characteristics of open and closed villages (Table 3) is not known and awaits further study. Another possibility, also unclear at present, is whether such townlands were 'open' or 'closed', or whether they just had 'open' or 'closed' landlords.

It is a truism accepted by historians that the Great Famine did not cause the social changes that occurred in the second half of the 19th century. Rather, what it did was to accelerate trends that were already underway.[4] One of these changes which, in Mayo, had started before the Famine was the change from the open-field (rundale) system of collective farming to a system of individual farms and fields that remains the norm today. Associated with this change was the demise of 'clachans', clusters of houses within the open-field system and their replacement with farmsteads. The timing of this change in farming systems is generally left vague but it is concluded from this study that, on the estate of Viscount Dillon in counties Mayo and Roscommon, it can be dated precisely from the Dillon estate maps in the National Library of Ireland. This is because, it is hypothesized, the maps were only drawn up when the system changed from rundale to individual farms, hence requiring a map of the individual holding of the tenants. If the hypothesis is correct, the Dillon estate was 'striped' between the early 1840s and the 1870s with most townlands converted to the new system in the period 1855 to 1859.

There was much hostility from the tenants to these changes. Some landlords claimed that this hostility was, in effect, just the fear of the unknown and, once the changes had been implemented, the tenantry would be more content, since it eliminated squabbles over allocation of land.[5] It is unclear whether the objections to these changes were due to the changes in the open-field system, or to the removal of the clachans. Whichever was the case, such changes must have created great tensions within the community, especially for those families who had survived the trauma of 'an gorta mór', the great hunger.

Clachans had been associated with communal violence and faction fighting throughout the 19th century in Ireland. Evidence is presented to show that such fighting occurred at Knock. Factions existed in the parish and some of the violence seems to have been factional. On other occasions the violence appeared to be religious and/or political in nature. Some of the events reported concerned attempted proselytization while, in other protests, demonstrators seemed to have financial motives, or long-held grievances. They were objecting to the payment of rent increases, tithes, or the priest's dues. Daniel Campbell used an odd phrase, to 21st-century ears, when he stated that the chapel at Knock 'was free' throughout the year except at Christmas and Easter when a collection was made at the eastern door.[6] It illustrates that even such small sums as the 2s. 2d. required to pay the priest his annual dues were a considerable financial burden on families that were just one or two steps from starvation.

All the events described above combined to create tension within the community, and tension was increased further in the late 1870s when another agricultural crisis occurred. The crop failures occurred throughout the country, but Co. Mayo was particularly badly affected. The hardship was the trigger which caused the land war to erupt in that part of the county, with the first demonstration occurring at Irishtown within a few miles of Knock. Tensions must have been at fever pitch when, just weeks later on 1 June 1879, thousands of angry tenants descended on the little village of Knock to protest against the priest and the landlords he was defending.

At that meeting the crowd shouted, 'three cheers for the Zulus.' The Anglo-Zulu war did not start until the British invaded Zululand on 11 January 1879, so the crowd were well aware of current national politics and world affairs.[7] Their awareness was, no doubt, gleaned from local newspapers such as the conservative *Mayo Constitution* or more likely the liberal *Connaught Telegraph* which was owned and edited by Mayo Tenants' Defence Association organizer, James Daly.[8] Both newspapers carried extensive coverage of world affairs, including events in Zululand, as well as full coverage of events in parliament. Thus, if historians of the 19th century wish to know what the people (of Knock or elsewhere) were thinking, they need to know what they were reading. If the protestors were reading about the Zulus (or having news read to them, if they could not read), then what else were they reading?

It has been demonstrated that nearly half of Knock's population was literate since before the Famine (Figure 6). So, were they aware of agrarian protests in Ireland or other parts of the kingdom, in earlier decades? Were they aware of the 'Swing riots' of the early 1830s, for example? E.P. Thompson comments on the influence of radical Irishmen, such as Ribbonmen, living in England, on agrarian protest in early 19th-century England.[9] It seems highly likely that Irish radicalism from the late 18th century influenced the English, but did it work the other way around? What were the precursors of the 'Rockite' protests seen in Knock in 1836? Were they the Captain Rock agitators from south-west Ireland in 1821–4, or were they Captain Swing's followers, who were causing havoc throughout southern England in the early 1830s?[10]

As Mokyr has shown in his study of the Famine, quantitative analysis of the data, such as ANOVA, can reveal relationships which would otherwise be obscure.[11] Conversely, without quantitative analysis, chance or random variation within the data can assume significance it does not deserve. Nowhere within this study have confidence levels or statistical analysis been applied to the data presented. However, despite this limitation, the results from this study could be used for comparative work in future research. The rise in literacy within the population of Knock during the 19th century could be compared to that of other parishes throughout Ireland, for example, and similarly with the decline in the use of the Irish language. Also, such analysis could allow for comparisons to be made of population changes on different estates which could inform any discussion of differences in the behaviour of landlords regarding their tenants.

It is hoped that the approach taken in this study, that of analysis at the parish or even the townland level, can be a useful tool for the historian of rural life in 19th-century Ireland. History awaits …

Appendix 1. Sources for census data, 1821–1901

Population and housing data contained in Table 2 and Figures 7 to 12 inclusive were obtained from the following sources:

1821 Census
Abstract of the answers and returns made pursuant to an act of the United Parliament, passed in the 55th year of the reign of his late majesty George the third, intituled, "an act to provide for taking an account of the population of Ireland, and for ascertaining the increase or diminution thereof." Preliminary observations. Enumeration abstract. Appendix. M. DCCC. XXI. (577), HC 1823, xxii, 411.

1831 Census
Population, Ireland. Abstract of answers and returns under the population acts, 55 Geo. III, chap. 120; 3 Geo. IV, chap. 5; 2 Geo. IV, chap. 30; 1 Will. IV, chap. 19. Enumeration 1831 (634), HC 1833, xxxix, 59.

1841–81 Censuses
Census of Ireland, 1881, part I, Area, houses and population: also the ages, civil or conjugal condition, occupations, birthplaces, religion, and education of the people, vol. IV, province of Connaught [C 3268] HC 1882, lxxix, 79.

1891 and 1901 Censuses
Census of Ireland, 1901, part I, Area, houses, and population: also the ages, civil or conjugal condition, occupations, birthplaces, religion, and education of the people, vol. IV, province of Connaught [Cd. 1059] HC 1902, cxxviii, 128.

Notes

ABBREVIATIONS

ANOVA	Analysis of variance
CP	Congregation of the Passion of Jesus Christ (Passionists)
CSORP	Chief Secretary's Office, Registered Papers
DED	District Electoral Division
IRB	Irish Republican Brotherhood
MP	Member of Parliament
NAI	National Archives of Ireland
NLI	National Library of Ireland
PP	Parish Priest
RC	Roman Catholic
RIC	Royal Irish Constabulary
TDA	Tenants' Defence Association
TFR	Total family reconstitution

ACKNOWLEDGMENTS

1 Francis J. Mayes, 'Land, landords and the Virgin Mary: rural tensions in Knock, County Mayo, in 1879' (MA thesis, NUI, Maynooth, 2020).

INTRODUCTION

1 See, for example: M.J. Winstanley, *Ireland and the land question, 1800–1922* (London, 1975); W.E. Vaughan, *Landlords and tenants in Ireland, 1848–1904* (Dundalk, 1984); Barbara Lewis Solow, *The land question in the Irish economy, 1870–1903* (Cambridge, 1971); Samuel Clark, *Social origins of the Irish Land War* (Princeton NJ, 1989); Paul Bew, *Land and the national question in Ireland, 1858–82* (Dublin, 1980).
2 J.S. Donnelly Jr, *The land and people of nineteenth-century Cork: the rural economy and the land question* (London, 1975); Donald Jordan, *Land and popular politics in Ireland: Country Mayo from the plantation to the Land War* (Cambridge, 1994).
3 *Connaught Telegraph,* 7 June 1879.
4 H. Carter to the Inspector General, 3 June 1879 (NAI, CSORP, 9632/1879).
5 For example: Pamela Sharpe, 'The total reconstitution method: a tool for class-specific study', *Local Population Studies,* 44 (1990), pp 41–51; or Peter Tilley, 'Creating life histories and family trees from nineteenth-century census records, parish registers and other sources', *Local Population Studies,* 68 (Spring 2002), pp 63–81.
6 Keith Wrightson and David Levine, *Poverty and piety in an English village, Terling, 1525–1700* (Oxford, 1995); Barry Reay, *Microhistories: demography, society and culture in rural England, 1800–1930* (Cambridge, 1996).
7 Daniel Campbell, Untitled memoir, typescript of a manuscript history of the parish of Knock, Co. Mayo, transcribed by Revd John Baptist Byrne 1900? (NLI, MS 31718), henceforth Campbell, untitled memoir.
8 Ibid., p. 7.
9 E. Pomfret, *The struggle for the land in Ireland, 1800–1923* (Princeton, 1930).
10 Solow, *The land question;* Donnelly, *The land and people.*
11 Ibid., pp 249–50.
12 Bew, *Land and the national question;* Clark, *Social origins.*
13 Jordan, *Land and popular politics.*

14 Ibid., p. 3.
15 Emmet Larkin, 'The devotional revolution in Ireland, 1850–75', *American Historical Review*, 77 (1972), pp 625–52.
16 R.F. Foster, *Modern Ireland, 1600–1972* (London, 1988), p. 386.
17 Colin Barr, 'The re-energizing of Catholicism, 1790–1880' in James Kelly (ed.), *The Cambridge history of Ireland, Volume 3* (Cambridge, 2018), p. 304.
18 Hynes, *Knock: the Virgin's apparition, see* Chapter 5, 'The people make a saint', pp 70–90.
19 Foster, *Modern Ireland*, p. 387.

I. THE 1901 CENSUS AS A SOURCE OF
19TH-CENTURY SOCIAL HISTORY

1 1901 Census of Ireland, County Mayo, Knock parish, Knock North, Knock South & Ballyhowly DEDs (NAI, viewed online at http://www.census.nationalarchives.ie/search/).
2 *Census of Ireland, 1901. Part I. Area, houses, and population: also the ages, civil or conjugal condition, occupations, birthplaces, religion, and education of the people, vol. IV, province of Connaught*, HC 1902 [Cd. 1059] CXXVIII, 128, Table XXIX.
3 A check of the parish register of Knock revealed at least three cases from among the families of Drum and Carrowmore townlands where subsequent children were named after dead siblings. In Carrowmore, for example, the family of Thomas Egan and his wife Mary (née Reynolds) baptized their son John on 18 May 1887. John died on the 8 May 1889, of whooping cough, and the couple's next child, a son, was baptized John the following month on 7 June.
4 1901 Census of Ireland, County Mayo, Knock parish, Knock North, Knock South & Ballyhowly DEDs, Form A (NAI, viewed online at http://www.census.nationalarchives.ie/search/).
5 Campbell, untitled memoir (NLI, MS 31718), p. 4.
6 1901 Census of Ireland, County Mayo, Knock parish, Knock North, Knock South & Ballyhowly DEDs, Form A (NAI, viewed online at http://www.census.nationalarchives.ie/search/).
7 Bridget Egan, aged 21, was their eldest daughter living with them. She spoke

English and Irish, but her 19-year-old sister, Maggie, and four younger children all spoke English only. The question of when bilingualism died out in the area is perhaps an area for future research.
8 The six enumerators of Knock parish recorded a total of 44 townlands. One of Knock's 45 townlands, Derryool, was uninhabited in 1901.
9 This categorization is based on that of Gary Crossley, 'Kinship and strategies for family survival on Bodmin Moor during the long nineteenth century (1793–1911)' (D.Phil., University of Oxford, 2017), pp 124–33 in order to make subsequent comparisons easier.

2. KNOCK, CO. MAYO IN THE 19TH
CENTURY

1 *Weekly Freeman's Journal*, 20 Sept. 1884.
2 Samuel Lewis, *A topographical dictionary of Ireland* (2 vols, Dublin, 1837), ii, p. 236.
3 Letter from Thomas O'Conor to Thomas A. Larcom written from Ballinrobe, Co. Mayo, concerning the history, topography and antiquities of the parishes of Annagh, Aghamore, Bekan and Knock, 16 August 1838 (Royal Irish Academy, Ordnance Survey of Ireland, OS Letters, Co. Mayo, vol. 2.
4 Ibid.
5 Hynes, *Knock: the Virgin's apparition*, p. 92.
6 Ibid., p. 92.
7 *Landowners in Ireland: Return of owners of land of one acre and upwards, in the several counties, counties of cities, and counties of towns in Ireland; showing the names of such owners arranged alphabetically in each county, their addresses as far as could be ascertained, the extent in statute acres and the valuation in each case; &c. &c. With a summary for each province and for all Ireland.* [C-1492], HL, 1876, XXIV, pp 83, 308, 315.
8 Henry Coulter, *The west of Ireland: its existing condition and prospects* (Dublin, 1862), p. 364.
9 Liam Swords, *In their own words: the famine in north Connacht, 1845–1849* (Dublin, 1999), p. 386.
10 Finley Dun, *Landlords and tenants in Ireland* (London, 1881), p. 203.
11 *Mayo Constitution*, 13 July 1847, p. 3.
12 Jordan, *Land and popular politics*, especially Demographic change in pre-Famine

Mayo, pp 118–30; S.H. Cousens, 'Emigration and demographic change in Ireland, 1851–1861', *Economic History Review*, 2nd Series, 14 (1961), pp 275–88.

13 Jordan, *Land and popular politics*, p. 123.

14 Hynes, *Knock: the Virgin's apparition*, footnote 10, p. 291.

15 Ibid., pp 95–6.

16 Campbell settled in the Smethwick district of Birmingham and is recorded in the 1851 census as living with his cousin (1851 Census of England, H.O. 107/2050 viewed online at: https://search.findmypast.co.uk). On 20 Nov. 1853 he married Hanora Brussell who was also born in Ireland, but it is not clear whether they met in Ireland or England (St Peter's Church, Broad St., Birmingham, parish register viewed online at https://www.ancestry.co.uk).

17 Campbell, untitled memoir (NLI, MS 31718).

18 Hynes, *Knock: the Virgin's apparition*, chapter 1, footnote 1, p. 267; Campbell, untitled memoir (NLI, MS 31718), introduction.

19 *Dublin Weekly Nation*, 6 Mar. 1880, p. 6; Burial register (St Phillip Neri RC Church, Smethwick, viewed online at https://search.findmypast.co.uk).

20 Hynes, *Knock: the Virgin's apparition*, pp 1–69.

21 Ibid., p. 96.

22 Campbell, untitled memoir (NLI, MS 31718), pp 22–3.

23 Hynes, *Knock: the Virgin's apparition*, p. 96.

24 Campbell, untitled memoir (NLI, MS 31718), p. 9.

25 Ibid., p. 10.

26 Robert Cruickshank, *Medical microbiology, a guide to the laboratory diagnosis and control of infection* (11th edition, revised reprint, Edinburgh and London, 1970), chapter 21, Cholera vibrio and allied organisms, pp 264–71.

27 Campbell, untitled memoir (NLI, MS 31718), p. 10.

28 Ibid.

29 Valuation revision books, 1858–1939 (Valuation Office Ireland, Co. Mayo, vol. 3, Ballyhowly, Co. Mayo, vol. 14, Knock North, & Co. Mayo, vol. 15, Knock South).

30 *Mayo Constitution*, 4 July 1854.

31 Richard Griffith, *General valuation of rateable property in Ireland, County of Mayo, valuation of the several tenements in the Union of Claremorris situated in the county above named* (Dublin, 1856), pp 60–2, 142–57. Henceforth *Griffith's Valuation*. I have included all townlands where the 'owner' was the immediate lessor in over ninety percent of the area of the townland, since in many townlands there were small areas sub-tenanted by other farmers. The two townlands owned by Thomas Nowlan, Cloondace and Drum, had reverted to Viscount Dillon's estate by 1860 where they remained for the rest of the century. They have therefore been included in that estate for this study.

32 Dennis Mills, *Lord and peasant in nineteenth-century Ireland* (London, 1980); B.A. Holderness, '"Open" and "close" parishes in England in the eighteenth and nineteenth centuries', *Agricultural History Review*, 20 (1972), pp 126–39.

33 Mills, *Lord and peasant*, p. 23.

34 Ibid., p. 24.

35 Kate Tiller, *An introduction to English local history* (2nd edition, Stroud, 2002), p. 221.

36 Mills, *Lord and peasant*, p. 117.

37 Tiller, *An introduction to English local history*, p. 222.

3. LAND, LANDLORDS AND TENANTS IN KNOCK DURING THE 19TH CENTURY

1 Frank Mitchell, *The Shell guide to reading the Irish landscape* (Dublin, 1986), figure 6.6 pp 176, 198.

2 E.E. Evans, *Irish folk ways* (London, 1957), pp 33–4.

3 Ibid., p. 29.

4 Evans, *Irish folk ways*, ibid.; David Hey (ed.), *The Oxford companion to family and local history* (Oxford, 2010), pp 391, 442, and see also R.H. Buchanan, 'Field systems in Ireland' in A.R.H. Baker and R.A. Butlin (eds), *Studies of field systems in the British Isles* (1973), cited by Hey, *Oxford companion*, p. 391.

5 Lord George Hill, *Gweedore: Facts from Gweedore* (1846; 5th edition, 1887), pp 22, 46, quoted by Evans, *Irish folk ways*, p. 24.

6 Evans, *Irish folk ways*, p. 24.

7 Jordan, *Land and popular politics*, p. 56.

8 Ibid., p. 57.

9 Michael Kelly, *Struggle and strife on a Mayo estate, 1833–1903. The Nolans of Logboy and their tenants,* Maynooth Studies in Local History, 116 (Dublin, 2014), p. 27.

10 Ibid., p. 18.

11 Ibid., pp 12, 13.

12 Coulter, *The west of Ireland*, p. 365.

13 *Maps of the estate of Viscount Dillon in County Mayo, by various surveyors, 3 volumes of large folio maps, coloured, and with names of tenants, 1842–75* (NLI, manuscript maps: 16 M 4–6).

14 Hill, *Gweedore*, p. 22, quoted by Evans, *Irish folk ways*, p. 24.

15 Dun, *Landlords and tenants*, pp 201–3.

16 Coulter, *The west of Ireland*, p. 365.

17 Dun, *Landlords and tenants*, p. 202.

18 Hill, *Gweedore*, p. 22, quoted by Evans, *Irish folk ways*, p. 32.

19 W.R. Wilde, *Dublin University Magazine*, 41 (1853), p. 20, cited by Evans, *Irish folk ways*, p. 32.

20 Evans, *Irish folk ways*, p. 32.

21 Tom Crehan, *Marcella Gerrard's Galway estate, 1820–70: 'awful extermination of tenantry'*, Maynooth Studies in Local History, 107 (Dublin, 2013), p. 34.

22 Ibid., p. 34.

23 Jordan, *Land and popular politics*, p. 147.

24 Ibid., p. 148.

25 Ibid., p. 149.

26 Ibid., p. 149.

27 Kelly, *Struggle and strife on a Mayo estate*, p. 12.

28 The 1948 play by M.J. Molloy, 'The king of Friday's men', is based on stories of Tulrahan faction fighting, recounted to Molloy by William Kelly, a Tulrahan resident. See Kelly, *Struggle and strife on a Mayo estate*, pp 12–13. See also: Michael Molloy, *Selected plays of M.J. Molloy, Irish drama selections 12* (Gerrards Cross, 1998), pp 1–84.

29 Evans, *Irish folk ways*, p. 31.

30 Campbell, untitled memoir (NLI, MS 31718), p. 1.

31 Ibid., p. 6.

32 Ibid., p. 7.

33 Ibid., p. 8.

34 *Mayo Constitution*, 7 July 1834.

35 Mary H. Thuente, 'Violence in pre-Famine Ireland: the testimony of Irish folklore and fiction', *Irish University Review*, 15:2 (Autumn, 1985), pp 129–47, at 136.

36 The story of the attack on Jeffers is taken from various newspapers' accounts of the three trials in which he featured: First trial, *Dublin Morning Register*, 27 July 1840, *Mayo Constitution*, 28 July 1840, *Tuam Herald*, 1 Aug. 1840; second trial, *Mayo Constitution*, 10 Aug. 1841; third trial, *Mayo Constitution*, 14 Mar. 1843.

37 *Dublin Morning Register*, 22 July 1840.

38 *Mayo Constitution*, 28 July 1840.

39 Ibid., 10 Aug. 1841.

40 Ibid., 14 Mar. 1843.

41 Ibid., 14 Mar. 1843.

42 Ibid., 18 Mar. 1836. Further details of this incident are given in the following week's issue of the paper: 25 Mar. 1836.

43 Campbell, untitled memoir (NLI, MS 31718), p. 18.

44 *Mayo Constitution*, 29 July 1835, and 22 Mar. 1836.

45 *Mayo Constitution*, 25 Feb. 1845.

46 Jordan, *Land and popular politics*, p. 146.

47 Ibid., pp 170–1.

48 Foster, *Modern Ireland*, p. 402.

49 Dublin Mansion House Committee for the Relief of Distress in Ireland, *J.A. Fox, member of the committee reports on the conditions of the peasantry of the county of Mayo, during the famine crisis of 1880* (Dublin, 1880), henceforth, Dublin Mansion House Committee, conditions of the peasantry.

50 Ibid., p. 10.

51 Ibid., p. 11.

52 Ibid., p. 26.

53 *Agricultural statistics, Ireland, 1879. Preliminary report on the returns of agricultural produce in Ireland in 1879, with tables,* [C. 2495], HC 1880, lxxxvi, 893, p. 48.

54 Dublin Mansion House Committee, conditions of the peasantry, p. 18.

55 Jordan, *Land and popular politics*, pp 206–7.

56 Ibid., pp 209–17.

57 Ibid., Chapter 6, pp 199–229.

58 Ibid., pp 217–21.

59 Ibid., p. 219.

60 *Connaught Telegraph*, 26 Apr. 1879.

61 Ibid., p. 5.

62 Jordan, *Land and popular politics*, Appendix 3, pp 324–8.

63 Names, as reported in the press, at this time are somewhat fluid. Cavanagh is sometimes spelt Kavanagh and O'Keane is also called O'Kane.

64 *Connaught Telegraph*, 31 May 1879.

65 Ibid., editorial.

66 *Connaught Telegraph*, 31 May 1879.

67 Ibid.

68 *Connaught Telegraph*, 7 June 1879.

69 H. Carter to The Inspector General, 3 June 1879 (NAI, CSORP, 9632/1879).

70 Liam Ua Catháin, *Venerable Archdeacon Cavanagh* (Dublin, 1953), p. 72.

71 Ibid., p. 73.

72 Ibid.

73 Paul Bew, 'A vision of the dispossessed? Popular piety and revolutionary politics in the Irish land war, 1879–82', in Judith Devlin and Ronan Fanning (eds), *Religion and rebellion* (Dublin, 1996), pp 137–51, p. 140.

74 *The Nation*, 6 March 1880.

CONCLUSION

1 William Shakespeare, *Henry the IV, part 2* (London, 1623), III.i.80.

2 For example, Donnelly, *The land and people of nineteenth-century Cork* (London, 1975); Donald Jordan, *Land and popular politics in Ireland: Country Mayo from the plantation to the Land War* (Cambridge, 1994).

3 Cousens, 'Emigration and demographic change', pp 278–82.

4 Foster, *Modern Ireland*, p. 318.

5 Coulter, *The west of Ireland*, p. 303.

6 Campbell, untitled memoir (NLI, MS 31718), p. 18.

7 For press reaction to the Anglo-Zulu war see Luke Diver, 'Perceptions versus reality? Newspaper coverage on the Anglo-Zulu war of 1879' (MA thesis, NUI, Maynooth, 2010).

8 For the rise of the local press during the 19th century in Ireland see: Marie-Louise Legg, *Newspapers and nationalism, the Irish provincial press, 1850–1892* (Dublin, 1999).

9 E.P. Thompson, *The making of the English working class* (London, 1963, 2013 Edition), pp 482–3.

10 E.J. Hobsbawm and George Rudé, *Captain Swing* (London, 1969).

11 Joel Mokyr, *Why Ireland starved: a quantitative and analytical history of the Irish economy, 1800–1850* (London, 1985).